PURPOSE POWER SECRETS

Exploring the Secrets to the Fulfillment of

God's

Original Intention for Man

SUNDAY A. EZEKIEL

Copyright © 2017 by: Sunday A. Ezekiel

Published in Nigeria by: DW-Impact Ltd, Lagos – Nigeria

All rights reserved. No portion of this publication may be reproduced, stored in retrieval system, or transmitted in any form by any means – electronic, mechanical, photocopying, recording, or any other – without the prior written permission of the publisher, except for brief quotations in printed reviews, magazines, articles etc.

For further enquiries, distribution or permission, contact:

Dreamers World Christian Centre

Phone: +234-8035122385, +234-7082982341

Email: info@dreamersworldng.org

Website: www.dreamersworldng.org

Facebook Pages: Dreamers World Christian Centre

Dream Big & Succeed Dreamers World International

All Scripture quotations are from the King James Version of the Bible, except otherwise stated.

CONTENTS

DEDICATION 7

FOREWORD 9

INTRODUCTION 13

Chapter 1: UNDERSTANDING GOD'S PURPOSE 21

Chapter 2: WHAT PURPOSE IS 38

Chapter 3: THE TRAGEDY OF UNDISCOVERED PURPOSE 59

Chapter 4: THE GLORY OF DISCOVERED PURPOSE 91

Chapter 5: DISCOVER YOUR GOD GIVEN PURPOSE 110

Chapter 6: PERSONAL PREPARATION DIMENSION 170

Chapter 7: DILIGENCE OF PURPOSE 212

Chapter 8: DISCIPLINE OF PURPOSE 246

Chapter 9: ASSOCIATION DIMENSIONS........... 281

Chapter 10: PATIENCE OF PURPOSE 314

Chapter 11: IT IS YOUR PROPHETIC ERA OF EXPLOITS 354

GET CONNECTED..367

Other Books By The Same Author.......................369

About The Author..370

DEDICATION

This book is dedicated to:

- God, my Father and the Sole Manufacturer of man;

- Jesus Christ, my Lord and King;

- The Holy Spirit, my teacher and the interpreter of the Manufacturer's manual;

- Dr. David Oyedepo, my father in the faith and mentor in ministry;

- All men who had discovered and fulfilled their God given purpose on earth;

- And all men who by reading this book will discover pursue and fulfill God's purpose for their lives.

FOREWORD

The subject of purpose is a very important one for anyone who hopes to be an achiever in life. Without purpose life would be lived aimlessly and carelessly and that is not God's design for us. God our creator is a God of purpose. There is nothing He has created that is purposeless. Anything in creation which, as human beings, we think is purposeless is because we have not yet discovered why God created it.

The discovery of purpose for which God has created each individual is the key to stardom on earth. There are no two people on earth today who have exactly the same purpose for which they are created and it is when each person discovers his true purpose on earth that he can become accomplished and also makes the world what God intends it to be.

It is one thing to discover ones purpose on earth and another to pursue it. It is actually the purpose discovered and pursued with tenacity that results in outstanding accolades. It is the purpose discovered and pursued that actually gladdens the heart of God our Creator.

It is tragic to note that a lot of people on earth today, including born again Christians, fail to realize the importance of discovering God's purpose for their lives let alone pursuing it. They therefore, fail to fulfill destiny as they go through life without making the world benefit from what God has designed them for.

In this book, the reader is made to understand what purpose is, the tragedy of undiscovered purpose and the blessings accruing from purpose discovered. Furthermore, great effort has been made to make the reader understand the difference between discovered purpose and purpose pursued. In addition, a lot of attention is devoted to all it would require to pursue ones discovered purpose.

Reading through this book, my conclusion is that it will stimulate the reader to discover the purpose for which God created him and that he can add value to the world particularly in the very area(s) that God made him to exist on the earth.

This book is very beautifully written in a style that is compelling to read. The author addresses the reader personally which makes it appear as if he (reader) is listening to a speech. Words of encouragement are also used frequently in the book to make the reader take necessary steps to actualize destiny and this makes it all the more unique.

I highly recommend this book to anyone who is keen on giving his life a meaning. I can assure you that anyone who picks up this book would never remain the same if he genuinely desires to positively impact the world as well as please God who has created him for a specific purpose on earth.

I wish you a happy and impactful reading.

Pastor Oluwole Olaoye

Living Faith Church

Canaanland

Nigeria

INTRODUCTION

You need to discover your assignment in life or you die in an asylum. - David Oyedepo

There is more to life than having educational qualifications, working in a multinational company, getting married and having children, building mansions and having the latest cars. There is more to life than heaping up money in the bank and having all manner of chieftaincy titles. Having all of these things is not what gives us meaning in life; they are just part of what God designed for us to have on earth. But to have meaning in life is to discover God's purpose for creating us; to locate the reason why we were sent to this world.

Nothing can be compared with God's purpose discovered and pursued by His creature. We are all products of divine purpose and until that purpose is discovered and pursued, there can not be any meaningful existence on earth.

God created all things; man, animal, plant and other things to add value to life. But value is provoked and released within the context of the purpose for which God created us.

God's perspective of success is directly opposite the world's definition of success. For instance, the world sees a successful man as one that has money in multimillion or multibillion; houses, cars, plenty of children, political position, chieftaincy title etc. That may be true to some level only if the man is living within the context of God's purpose for his life; because God's definition of success, which is the most authentic definition is for a man to live his life according to God's purpose for him with or without all those things mentioned above.

Luke 12:15;

And he said unto them, take heed, and beware of covetousness: for a man's life consisteth not in the abundance of the things which he possesseth.

We need to understand that what we possess in life is not what defines our values. Real life and effective living on earth is defined by your discovery and pursuit of divine purpose; it is by your correct positioning with God's ordained plan for your life.

As a student of life issues, I have seen multibillionaires who rather than add value have contributed to a lot of evils in the world with the money they have. This is because material and financial possessions not utilized in line with divine purpose become sources of crisis in the world.

We have heard of civil and political wars in recent times in different nations of the world as a result of selfish ambitions of political leaders who have turned governance to an institution for amassing wealth for selfish interests. If these people had chosen to discover and pursue divine purpose even as political leaders, they would have added great value to life instead of becoming perpetrators of evil in their nations leading to the death of thousands of their own citizens.

You are born to add value to life by finding meaning for your life through divine purpose. Do not misjudge yourself; you carry a heavenly mandate on your life and you cannot afford to go to the grave without fulfilling that divine mandate here on earth.

This book is the outcome of the discovery of God's purpose for my life after years of intense study and search for meaning in life. When I found it, I determined not to die with God's purpose unfulfilled and His potentials in me unreleased. I decided that I will not add to the wealth in the cemetery of the world. I chose to make my own contributions to life by a tireless pursuit of His purpose for me as I help others in discovering what heaven has deposited in them before the foundation of the world.

Dr. Myles Munroe once said; **"Nothing is worse than being alive and not knowing why."**

Friend, you may look like nobody now, but understand that everyone who became 'somebody' today were sometimes ago a 'nobody'. The truth about you is that, you can make a difference in the world by discovering and pursuing your purpose. When you find your unique assignment in life, you are on your way to adding value to your world.

It is not a coincidence that you are reading this book; I believe that it is ordained that now is the time for you to rise from obscurity into the limelight in life. You are a blessing to this world and your perspective about life must change after reading through this book.

You are very important to God's agenda as a blessing to your generation. Destinies of born and unborn children are tied to the discovery of your own divinely ordained purpose. I believe that your name and your space will not be empty in the museum of great achievers in the world.

Chapter 1: UNDERSTANDING GOD'S PURPOSE

Definiteness of purpose is the starting point of all achievement.

W. Clement Stone

Success in life is only guaranteed within the context of divine purpose.

Sam Adeyemi

Let us begin by looking at God's perspective about understanding. The best place we can get the truth is from God's Word; because the beginning is the best place to begin in order to end well.

Proverbs 21:16;

The man that wandereth out of the way of understanding shall remain in the congregation of the dead.

Lack of understanding lead to spiritual, intellectual and physical death

Psalm 82:5;

They know not, neither will they understand; they walk on in darkness: all

the foundations of the earth are out of course.

Lack of understanding puts one in darkness.

Acts 8:30-31;

And Philip ran thither to him, and heard him read the prophet Esaias, and said, Understandest thou what thou readest?

And he said, How can I, except some man should guide me? And he desired Philip that he would come up and sit with him.

Lack of understanding takes people to hell after death.

God's perspective about understanding shows that profitability is a product of understanding. You cannot benefit much from a product, no matter how powerful it is if you do not have an in-depth understanding of the product. That means, your level of understanding is what determines how outstanding your result will be in life.

Every outstanding result is at the command of good understanding and the more your understanding, the greater the result you command.

Your understanding level determines your limit in life because understanding is what gives value to life. It then suffices to conclude that in the absence of understanding, death ensues according to Proverbs 21:16 as quoted above.

Therefore, understanding the subject of purpose is very crucial to your fulfillment in life.

Everything in life is controlled and governed by the power of purpose. Nothing exists on earth without a peculiar purpose. Just as no one embarks on any project without a specific reason for doing so, in the same way, God never went into production until He had concluded the purpose that His products would serve on earth. Everything in life exists for a specific purpose. Therefore, you are a product of purpose.

When you do not know the purpose of a product, all you will do is to abuse it.

Dr. Myles Munroe once said; *"When purpose is not known, abuse is inevitable."*

To abuse something is to use it abnormally. As a matter of fact, the word 'abuse' came from a combination of two words; abnormal and use. So 'abuse' simply means; abnormal usage of a thing.

At the root of every form of frustration in life is lack of understanding of purpose. The glory of a man is in the fulfillment of God's purpose for his life.

It was Dr. Martin Luther King Jnr. that said; *"If a man has no purpose for living, he is not fit to live."*

That statement shows that everyman has a purpose, but only very few understand what it means; and only a small fraction of the very few have actually discovered their God ordained purposes for living.

As a child of God, you must not mistake existence for living. Real life and effective living is found in the discovery and pursuit of your purpose. Until that is settled, life remains a mere existence; an experiment.

God is a God of purpose. He does nothing for entertainment or for beautification; rather, He created all things for specific purposes. And because you are created in His image and likeness; therefore, you are a product of purpose.

THE POWER OF PURPOSE

Proverbs 19:21;

Many are the plans in a man's heart, but it is the LORD's purpose that prevails. (NIV)

I want you to read that scriptural statement above several times and pay very close attention to each of the words.

This statement was made by King Solomon; a man who was reputed to be the wisest man in his days. I believe there is a lot of wisdom for us to learn from this statement.

King Solomon brought out the relationship existing between man's plans and God's purpose, and we can see the power that the latter has over the former. According to this statement, no matter what plans man may have, the purpose of God will always prevail over the plans of man. In other words, God's purpose for man must be discovered before any plan made by man can become meaningful. God's purpose has no respect for man's plans because His purpose precedes man's plans.

Just as you cannot make your own plan for a product except it falls in line with the manufacturer's purpose for it, in the same way, you cannot make any satisfactory plans for your life without submitting to the purpose for which your manufacturer, God has created you.

Rick Warren, the author of The Purpose Driven Life said; **"If you're alive, there's a purpose for your life"**.

In case, life appears tough and meaningless and it looks like things are not working for you, try to find out if you are living in line with God's purpose for your life. It may be that all you are doing is pursuing your own plans at the expense of God's purpose for you. I believe that God will give you the revelation of His divine purpose for you as you read on. You will locate where you belong in destiny, because you are at your best when you are in your heavenly ordained place.

Ambition cannot take you to your place of fulfillment; only divine purpose - discovered and pursued - can. Your ambition is what you want to do in life; but purpose is what God has created you to do in life. And God's purpose for you will prevail over your ambition.

Also, from that statement of King Solomon, Proverbs 19:21, as quoted above, it is revealed that purpose is more important to God than plans, it is more powerful than plans and it always precedes plans.

God's purpose is what summarizes His priority, motivation and commitment to His products. God's commitment to His purpose for you is greater than His commitment to your plans, except if your plan is consistent with His purpose for creating you. The only thing that matters to God after your salvation experience is His purpose for creating you.

Isaiah 46:9-10;

Remember the former things, those of long ago; I am God, and there is no other; I am God, and there is none like me. I make known the end from the beginning, from ancient times, what is still to come. I say: My Purpose Will Stand, And I Will Do All That I Please. (NIV)

The purpose of God for your life will stand no matter what plans you have made for yourself. God set you apart for something specific on earth. But it is your responsibility to locate yourself within the center of that specific purpose. God will ensure that what He has created you for prevails over whatever you plan to do.

You are not a biological accident; neither are you a product of happenstance. You are here on earth for a specific and peculiar reason; it is within the context of that reason that your life can have a meaning.

Viktor Frankl once said; "The need to find meaning in life is more basic to a human being than pleasure or power or anything else. If a person has a 'why' to live, he can endure almost anyhow. But if that dimension of 'why' is lacking, then the whole structure of one's life eventually collapses."

The Prophet Jeremiah was told by God in Jeremiah 1:5;

Before I formed you in the womb I knew you, before you were born I set you apart; I appointed you as a prophet to the nations. (NIV)

Also, the great Apostle, Paul affirmed concerning himself in his epistle to the Galatians church as recorded in

Galatians 1:15;

But when it pleased God, who separated me from my mother's womb, and called me by his grace.

God knew you; He chose you; He predestined you and He set you apart, before the foundation of the world, in order to fulfill a peculiar purpose on earth. The same way He separated Prophet Jeremiah and Apostle Paul according to the two scriptures above, you and I were also separated by God unto specific purpose to fulfill on earth; this is because God has not changed and He cannot change. (Malachi 3:6)

You were separated from your mother's womb as a blessing to the world. But this can only become real by discovering and pursuing your God ordained purpose on earth. You matter to God's end time agenda. The world needs you at such a time as this. That is why you are kept alive by God. Therefore, you must be determined not to die with God's purpose unfulfilled.

Elisabeth Kubler-Ross said; **"Learn to get in touch with the silence within yourself, and know that everything in life has purpose. There are no mistakes, no coincidences, all events are blessings given to us to learn from."**

You need to accept responsibility to discover, pursue and fulfill your God ordained purpose and you will be glad for obeying God at the end of your life. You have just one life to live and you cannot afford to live that one life anyhow. I see you ending up a fulfilled person at the end of your time on earth.

Chapter 2: WHAT PURPOSE IS

Purpose is what gives life a meaning. - Charles H. Perkhurst

I have brought myself, by long meditation, to the conviction that a human being with a settled purpose must accomplish it, and that nothing can resist a will which will stake even existence upon its fulfillment. - Benjamin Disraeli

Purpose is a very important subject of life that all need to pay full attention to. It is not the best for us to assume that what will happen will happen, neither is it noble for anyone to think that people will always become what they wanted to become in life.

I have found out by research that about eighty to ninety percent of the human population is not positioned in the center of God's purpose for their life. The reason for this is that people lack the adequate knowledge of what purpose is.

And when you are ignorant of what God has created you for; you will not give yourself to any meaningful pursuit in life. If you live outside of divine purpose, you will not be fulfilled in life.

Our decisions in life are the determinants of all that happen to us in life. If you decide to discover and pursue your life purpose, you will become exactly what you pursue. It is your decision that creates your future.

WHAT IS PURPOSE?

According to Oxford Dictionary of Current English, purpose means; object to be attained, thing intended, intention to act, resolution, determination, intended result of effort.

The word intention means what was in the mind before an action is carried out or implemented.

I want to define purpose as;

the reason why a thing was made,

the end that started the beginning,

the intended result about a thing,

the expected end of a thing,

the motivation for creation,

the commitment of a manufacturer about his product, something set up as an object or end to be attained.

Basically, your purpose is the end goal that drives your current actions. It's the reason that you work on the things you do, the outcome you wish to achieve by your efforts.

Now, drawing from the definitions above, we can relate it to God the creator and Sole Manufacturer and man His creature and product. In the light of that relationship, we can conclude that;

Purpose is God's original intention for creating man.

Purpose is the reason why God made man.

Purpose is God's motivation for manufacturing man.

Purpose is God's intended result for which He created man.

Purpose is God's established end for which man was started.

What this means is that, no man on earth today exist without a particular intention in God's mind before the creation. It is what God had in mind as His purpose for man that necessitated man's creation. God has a peculiar purpose for every man and whether that purpose is fulfilled or not depends on man's decision to understand, discover and pursue that purpose of God for creating him.

Michel de Montaigne once said; *"**The soul which has no fixed purpose in life is lost; to be everywhere, is to be nowhere.**"*

It is God's purpose for man that determine His priority, motivation and commitment to man. No manufacturer will ever go into production without first establishing what purpose his product will perform. And in the same way, God created man according to the purpose He had in mind for man before the foundation of the world.

Success in life is the fulfillment of the original intent or purpose established by the manufacturer of a product or the initiator and source of an assignment. You cannot measure your success by comparing what you have done in life with what others have done; rather, your success is measured by comparing what you have done with what you are created to do. In God's perspective, a man is a success when he has fulfilled divine purpose, no matter what other things he might have done.

Your life's purpose is the original intent or predetermined result of God for you; it is God's expected end for you. The only true source of definition for anything in life is the original purpose for its existence.

Purpose: The Big Picture

The most important thing in life is the big picture, and it is purpose that defines the big picture. That big picture is the original purpose or intent of the manufacturer or originator of an event; it is the desired end result. Without this big picture which is the purpose of God for creating man, human life has no meaning or significance. Therefore, if our lives are to have meaning, we must recover the big picture of God's original intent for us.

I like the way Robert Byrne puts it when he said;

"The purpose of life is a life of purpose."

The discovery and recovery of the big picture is an individual's personal responsibility. This is because, a man who becomes conscious of the responsibility he bears toward a human being who affectionately waits for him, or to an unfinished work, will never be able to throw away his life. He knows the 'why' for his existence, and will be able to bear almost any 'how.'

To begin with, ask yourself these questions;

'What am I involved in right now?'

'What is my reason for doing what I am doing?'

'What is my original intention as designed by God, my creator?'

Do not think that you can do anything you decide to do and become a success; your success is determined only by the purpose of God for creating you. If what you are involved in right now is not consistent with what God has created you for, then you need to take the time to find out from God who created you what He has created you to do on earth.

When you discover your purpose, you will never try to be like someone else. The best you can become is you. You are created an original; the only number one you. If you try to be like someone else, you end up as number two of that person and you lose you own identity.

You can learn from people and be inspired by them in your bid to fulfill your purpose, but you cannot be like anybody else. Just be yourself and line yourself up with God's original intention for you and then your success in life is sure.

THE BENEFITS OF DISCOVERY OF PURPOSE

When you discover God's purpose for your life, you experience unusual benefits among which are:

PEACE

When you are in the centre of God's purpose, you are at peace no matter the challenges that may come your way. This is because; nothing can stand against the fulfillment of what God has concluded before the foundation of the world.

Purpose exists before creation and purpose is what forces creation; that is why the understanding of the truth about purpose brings you peace. You are too sure to see the fulfillment of divine purpose because nothing can work against the truth.

Jesus was at peace at every stage of His assignment on earth because He knew the purpose of God for His life. As a matter of fact, He emphasized the purpose of His coming to earth in several aspects of the scripture.

John 6:38;

For I have come down from heaven not to do My own will and purpose but to do the Will and Purpose of Him who sent me. (AMP)

John 18:37;

Pilate replied, "But you are a king then?" "Yes," Jesus said. "I was born for that Purpose. And I came to bring truth to the world. All who love the truth are my followers." (TLB)

Luke 4:43;

But He said to them, I must preach the good news (the Gospel) of the kingdom of God to the other cities [and towns] also, for I was sent for this [purpose]. (AMP)

When you get to the knowledge of why you are sent to this world, peace becomes your companion. You will never know fear of any kind, because God's purpose will stand in your life.

A FOCUSED LIFE

With the knowledge of your purpose, your life will be focused on the fulfillment of that purpose. You will not be going from place to place. You will know what to concentrate your life on. There is only one purpose God had in mind for creating you. When you are not focused on one thing that God created you for, you cannot become fulfilled in anything.

It was Anthony Robbins that said *"One reason so few of us achieve what we truly want is that we never direct our focus; we never concentrate our power. Most people dabble their way through life, never deciding to master anything in particular."*

Discovery of your purpose makes you focus you spiritual, physical and mental resources and you will be able to solve problem for the world with a focused lifestyle.

1 Corinthians 6:12;

All things are Lawful unto me, but all things are not expedient: all things are lawful for me, but I will not be brought under the power of any.

When you know your purpose on earth, you will be able to distinguish between what is lawful and what is expedient; what is permissible and what is beneficial. You are not born to do everything. You are born for just one purpose and that is where your fulfillment lies. Purpose makes life simple because it helps you maintain a focused life.

Therefore, it is time to gather in your resources, rally all your faculties, marshal all your energies, and focus all your capacities upon mastery of all the things you need to fulfill that one purpose for which God has created you.

PROSPERITY

The knowledge of your purpose in life brings you into a prosperous life. In my study of great and prosperous men on earth, I have come discover that they are men of purpose with focus. Men who have discovered God's purpose and focused on its pursuit do not crave for wealth. They naturally become prosperous as they pursue divine purpose. The provision of God will always flow in the direction of His purpose. As you pursue your known purpose, the resources needed for the tasks will always flow to you.

One thing I have come to find out is that poverty is a direct product of man's ignorance of his divine purpose or disobedience to the pursuit of divine purpose. When you discover and pursue your purpose, you make satisfactory progress and flow in God's prosperity plan for your life.

Job 36:11;

If they obey and serve him, they shall spend their days in prosperity, and their years in pleasures.

The discovery and pursuit of your purpose is obedience to God. In pursuing that purpose, you are serving Him and mankind, then, you are covenant bound to spend your days in prosperity and pleasure.

ALL ROUND VICTORY

When you are in the centre of God's purpose for your life, all things will work in your favour. No matter what challenge that confronts you, you will always be victorious, because God is committed to ensuring that His purpose for your life becomes a reality.

Your purpose is what God ordained for you before you were born and your calling into this world is according to His purpose for you, therefore, everything on earth will work out in your favour (Romans 8:28-30)

As long as you are in the pursuit of His purpose for your life, your ways will be pleasing to God and all things will be at peace with you.

Proverbs 16:7;

When a man's ways please the LORD, he maketh even his enemies to be at peace with him.

Purpose is the key to success and fulfillment of destiny is in discovery and pursuit of that one purpose of God for man. Every thing is created for a peculiar purpose. You will get to the full realization of what heaven has sent you on earth to do in Jesus Name.

Chapter 3: THE TRAGEDY OF UNDISCOVERED PURPOSE

The wealthiest spot on earth is not the oil field of Iraq, neither is it the gold mine of the world, but it is the cemetery. - Myles Munroe

The end result of every purpose not discovered or not pursued is tragedy. The word tragedy means; serious accident, disaster or sad event. It means a situation where one is dealing with a tragic event that ends unhappily.

It is tragic for a man not to discover his purpose in life. In other words, when people fail to discover and pursue their God ordained purpose on earth, it is a sad event; a disaster and a serious accident.

Please understand that death is not the most tragic event in life. Undiscovered purpose is more tragic than death. Although God destined us to live long on earth, but He is more interested in us living the life of His purpose while we are on earth, not just to live long and die unfulfilled.

The grave yard of the world is filled with undiscovered destinies and visions that were never fulfilled. This is because men die young or even at very good old age without discovering their God given purpose. They die unfulfilled. They go back to the grave with what God put in them to be released to bless the world. The tragedy is not their death, but their undiscovered and unreleased God-given purpose.

God is happy with us when we do the exact thing He created us to do. Any product of any manufacturer that does not conform to the purpose for which the manufacturer made it brings concern to the manufacturer. Such product is categorized as a failed product.

You are a product of God, the Sole Manufacturer of man. He is committed to the fulfillment of the purpose for which He has created you, but it is your responsibility to discover and pursue that purpose. When you do not fulfill the purpose for which you were created, it is a tragedy.

You are not to add to the wealth in the cemeteries of the world. You must deliver what God has deposited in you for the benefit of mankind.

I believe that through your encounters in this book, your name will not be part of the list of those whose visions and dreams had perished in the grave yards of the world. Your life will not end in tragedy because you will die empty with your purpose fully fulfilled at the end of your life.

I want to use two products as examples to reveal how tragic it is when purpose is not discovered and pursued.

A car bought but left unused, not serviced for years, but abandoned in the garage is not fulfilling the purpose for which the manufacturer made it. That car was built with a specific purpose as specified by the manufacturer. Every components and parts of the car was assembled together by the manufacturer so that it can fulfill the purpose of moving people and/or goods from place to place. The engine was designed to be ignited so that the gasoline and oil will circulate to the appropriate places so as to enhance its proper operation. The body was built to be able to hold the interior together as one single entity called a car.

That same car that was designed for this noble function becomes useless when it is not used for its purpose. That is a tragedy.

Another example is a house built and abandoned for years, not inhabited by people, it begins to deteriorate faster and loses it value, because it is not fulfilling the purpose for which it was built. That is another tragedy of unfulfilled purpose.

It is a well known fact that every divine deposit multiplies by reason of use. When something precious is left unused it cannot fulfill its purpose. You owe God the responsibility of discovering and pursuing His purpose for your life so that you do not end up in tragedy.

The man Saul, who later became Apostle Paul, was living in tragedy ignorantly before he met Jesus on his way to carrying out his tragic mission in Damascus. Thank God for His mercy on him, if not

Saul would have ended his life in tragedy; purpose not discovered.

Saul was living contrary to the purpose for which God gave him life and he was ignorant of this. He was busy living against his heavenly mandate because he had not discovered it. Can you see how important this issue is to us?

Ignorance of divine purpose results in man's destruction. When you are ignorant of your divine purpose, you run wild; that is, you live your life any how without meaning. And if you live any how you end up any how. That is not God's intention for you and all His creatures.

Just imagine how Saul (Paul) would have ended his life if he had not discovered God's purpose for his life.

He was practically involved in the murder of Stephen. Can you imagine someone destined by God to be a great Apostle to the body of Christ been part of the killing of God's messenger? (Acts 7:58).

He even went ahead to obtain a letter of authority from the priest to humiliate Christians in Damascus for no just cause, all because he was ignorant of his God-given purpose. (Acts 9:1-2)

That shows how tragic it is when purpose is not known. Saul was just zealous about his so called

Jewish law and as a well informed lawyer; he believed he was doing what was right.

The same Saul, now Apostle Paul encountered God on his journey to Damascus. That singular encounter was the turning point in his life, because that same encounter delivered to him his God given purpose in life (Acts 9:3-7).

Now after many years and series of encounters with God, Saul, now Apostle Paul referred to himself as one set apart from his mother's womb and called for a specific purpose.

Galatians 1:15-16;

But when it pleased God, who separated me from my mother's womb, and called me by his grace,

To reveal his Son in me, that I might preach him among the heathen; immediately I conferred not with flesh and blood.

Despite all the evil things that Paul did, God had already set him apart for a specific purpose as a preacher of the New Testament and great evangelist from the foundation of the world.

Everything about Paul changed when he met with divine purpose. He began to live a different life from the previous one. What a tragedy it would have been if he never met with divine purpose?

Friend, many people living on earth today are living in tragedy, because they are yet to discover divine purpose. You must remove your name from that list as you make up your mind to discover your God given purpose and stick your life to its pursuit.

You cannot have a disciplined life until you discover you purpose. It is your discovery that will dictate your lifestyle and the direction to which you are moving in life. When you find purpose, you will always know what to do, where to go and how to live. You will be a man of impact when you find your purpose. As a matter of fact, the transformations and revolutions we have experienced in the world so far are direct result of fulfillment of God's purpose discovered and pursued by men.

For instance, it was when Paul discovered his purpose that the door of the gospel opened to the gentiles because that was why he was created by God. How would it have been if Paul died without discovering that purpose? May be the gentiles would not have been privileged to gain access to the gospel of Jesus. That would have been a great tragedy, because, purpose not discovered and pursued results in tragedy in life.

The same Paul wrote about half of the New Testament and he singlehandedly did more exploits in his 38 years of ministry than any denomination had done in 500 years before him.

In the past, great inventors and leaders such as Michael Faraday, Albert Einstein, Thomas Edison, The Wright brothers, Isaac Newton, Henry Ford, Alexander Graham Bell, Martin Luther King Jnr et cetera were men who changed the course of history and transformed the world as a result of the discoveries and tireless pursuits of their God given purposes on earth. Although they all died long ago, their discoveries are still speaking and blessing the world today.

Just imagine where the world would have been today without electricity, automobile, aircraft, telecommunication et cetera. How would we live the way we are living now? How would we travel from nation to nation, continent to continent without aircrafts? How could we communicate over a long distance without telephones?

With the internet technology, the world has become a 'global village' where we can share information and ideas from nation to nation without having to travel. All these were discoveries of men who refused to die and add the treasures in them to the wealth in the cemeteries of the world.

The cemetery is wealthy enough so you do not have to contribute to its wealth. Only God can fathom how wealthy the cemeteries of the world are because many great inventions and discoveries of men never saw the light of the day. Only God can tell the number of ideas, books, businesses, ministries and many great inventions of men that have perished in the grave yard of the world.

The invention of electricity by Michael Faraday has brought great revolution to the world. This is a product of the discovery of God's purpose for his existence on earth.

Faraday established the basis for the electromagnetic field concept in physics. He similarly discovered electromagnetic induction, diamagnetism, and laws of electrolysis. He established that magnetism could affect rays of light and that there was an underlying relationship between the two phenomena. His inventions of electromagnetic rotary devices formed the foundation of electric motor technology, and it was largely due to his efforts that electricity became viable for use in technology worldwide.

Can you imagine a world where there was no electricity? If Faraday did not discover it before he died, his death would have been a tragedy because he would have added this great world changing invention to the wealth in the grave yard. Faraday died a fulfilled man because his discoveries are still speaking today. The world of science changed by his many other inventions.

Biographers have noted that **"a strong sense of the unity of God and nature"** pervaded Faraday's life and work. I believe this was what helped him to discover what he was created by God to do on earth.

Another tragedy that never was is the discovery of the Law of gravity by Isaac Newton among many others of his discoveries which came by observation. Newton's law of gravity was a major landmark in science revolution.

In this work, he described universal gravitation and the three laws of motion, which dominated the scientific view of the physical universe for the next three centuries. Newton showed that the motions of objects on Earth and of celestial bodies are governed by the same set of natural laws, by demonstrating the consistency between Kepler's laws of planetary motion and his theory of gravitation; thus removing the last doubts about heliocentrism and advancing the Science Revolution.

Newton built the first practical reflecting telescope and developed a theory of colour based on the observation that a prism decomposes white light into the many colours that form the visible spectrum. He also formulated an empirical law of cooling and studied the speed of sound.

Newton was also highly religious. He was an unorthodox Christian, and wrote more on Biblical hermeneutics than on science and mathematics, the subjects he is mainly associated with. He is considered by many scholars and members of the general public to be one of the most influential people in human history. And he died as a man who fulfilled divine purpose.

Sir Alexander Graham Bell, the inventor of telephone was another purpose-driven man. His initial work on the harmonic telegraph had entered a formative stage with progress it made both at his new Boston "laboratory" (a rented facility) as well as at his family home in Canada a big success. While working that summer in Brantford, Bell experimented with a ***"phonautograph"***, a pen-like machine that could draw shapes of sound waves on smoked glass by tracing their vibrations.

Bell thought it might be possible to generate undulating electrical currents that corresponded to sound waves. Bell also thought that multiple metal reeds tuned to different frequencies like a harp would be able to convert the undulatory currents back into sound. But he had no working model to demonstrate the feasibility of these ideas.

On March 10, 1876, three days after his patent was issued, Bell succeeded in getting his telephone to work, using a liquid transmitter similar to Gray's design. Vibration of the diaphragm caused a needle to vibrate in the water, varying the electrical resistance in the circuit.

The Bell Telephone Company was created in 1877, and by 1886 over 150,000 people in the U.S. owned telephones. Bell company engineers made numerous other improvements to the telephone, which emerged as one of the most successful products ever.

In January 1915, Bell made the first ceremonial transcontinental telephone call. Calling from the AT&T head office at 15 Dey Street in New York City, Bell was heard by Thomas Watson at 333 Grant Avenue in San Francisco.

Today telephone is used world wide and it has added great value to people and how we do business globally, because the man refused to add his treasures to the wealth in the grave yard.

Friend, imagine the tragedy that would have resulted in the world if these men failed to discover what God has deposited in them. They are blessings to the world because they discovered and fulfilled their God given purpose on earth. Although, they died long ago, their purpose fulfilled speaks on for life.

A wise man said; **"Necessity is the mother of invention."** In other words, your discovery is an invention of what will bring solution to the world. Therefore, choose not to go to the grave yard with it. God puts it in you for the purpose of blessing the world.

In the Christian world, that is, the church, we have witnessed great advancements by virtue of the discovery of God-given purpose by men. Great preachers and teachers such as John Wesley, Smith Wigglesworth, Billy Graham, Kenneth E. Hagin, Enoch Adeboye, David Oyedepo, Myles Munroe, Kenneth Copeland etc. are men that are making global impact through the discovery of their God ordained purpose on earth.

The message of faith which characterize the life and ministries of these great men has brought about salvation of souls in hundreds of million, healings, deliverances and prosperity to people. A great number of people have found hope, joy, health and discovery of divine purpose through their discovered and pursued purpose, which became their ministries.

Also, many great schools, hospitals and other life transforming ventures have been built by the ministries of these men. I cannot imagine what Christianity would have been today if these men had not discovered their God given purposes and pursued them. That would have been great tragedy in the world.

Friend, you are next in line to become a blessing to the world as you discover and fulfill your purpose in life. You are not different from these men; it is just that you are yet to discover your own God given purpose or that you are in the process of its fulfillment.

If you want the world to talk about you for good tomorrow, it is the discovery of your God given purpose that will make it happen. God has ordained that all His children will become solutions to the world's problems by virtue of His purpose for creating them. Therefore, my questions to you are; what do you want to be remembered for when your time on earth is over? What values are you suppose to add to the world?

These questions can only be answered by the discovery and pursuit of your purpose.

The purpose-drive man, Benjamin Franklin once said; ***"If you want to be remembered when you are dead and rotten, either do things worth writing or write things worth reading."***

Few years ago, David, the Psalmist was remembered 3,000 years after he named Jerusalem, the City of David. Men of purpose do not die because their discoveries and deliveries continued to live on in blessing mankind.

In some years to come, will the world still remember that you came to this earth the way we remember the great, purpose-drive man I have discussed above? Your discovered and fulfilled purpose is the only thing that will make that happen.

Posterity will not forgive you if you fail to deliver what God has created you to release as a blessing to the world before you time is over. The time for that is now. No matter how old you are now, the time is always right to do the right thing and now is the time. You cannot afford to end your life in tragedy.

For instance, David began at a very young age of sixteen years when he was anointed to be a king and he fulfilled his purpose before he died at seventy years old. And fulfilled God's purpose for his life that is why the whole world still talks about his great accomplishments today. (Acts 13:36-37).

Also, Abraham the father of faith began his life at the age of 75 when God called him. Irrespective of how advanced in age he was when he found God's purpose for his life, he ended up as a fulfilled man at a very good old age. (Genesis 24:1-2)

Abraham ended up being the example of the faith movement on earth and he fulfilled his God given purpose at a well advanced age.

Understand that God has called you to this earth for a unique assignment. It is your responsibility to find it and stick with its pursuit so that you do not end in tragedy. Purpose not discovered and pursued equals destiny aborted. And when there is an abortion of any kind, it results in tragedy.

However, you are not only to discover and pursue your purpose, but to finish the work that God sent you here to do. But how are you going to finish what you did not discover and/or pursue?

Apostle Paul, a man of great exploits with fulfilled purpose at end of his life said that he has finished his assignment.

2 Timothy 4:6-7;

As for me, my life has already been poured out as an offering to God. The time of my death is near.

I have fought a good fight, I have finished the race, and I have remained faithful. (NLT)

What a great joy that this man who was living a wild, meaningless life at the beginning of his life ended by affirming that he had finished the work God gave him to do on earth? You know that he would not have been able to make that statement if he did not discover and pursue God's purpose for him.

Also, earlier before Paul came on the scene of discovery and fulfillment of purpose, Jesus made that statement when He completed the work of redemption for mankind on the cross. Since He completed the object of God's purpose for Him, He died a fulfilled man.

John 19:30;

When Jesus therefore had received the vinegar, he said; it is finished: and he bowed his head, and gave up the ghost.

Friend, I rejoice with you because I believe that at the end of your time on earth, you will say like Jesus and Paul; "I have finished my cause".

I believe that by the time you are through reading this book, you will not only know how to discover your God given purpose on earth, you will also know what it takes to fully fulfill and finish your assignment. God will reveal to you your destiny by the help of the Spirit and He will empower you to obey and take the steps of faith required so that you can finish strong.

I will conclude this chapter with what the great man of God, Kenneth E. Hagin wrote in his book Plans, Purposes And Pursuits; ***"Dear friends, if you are too busy to wait on God to discover His plan, you may go through your entire life and everything you do will be in vain. Then what will you say to God when you stand*** *before Him in eternity? He won't ask you about those things you did according to your ideas and plans. He will want to know what you did about His plan for your life."*

Chapter 4: THE GLORY OF DISCOVERED PURPOSE

When purpose is known, glory is revealed, but ignorance of purpose equals abortion of destiny. - Sunday A. Ezekiel

I believe that now, it has become very clear to you that the best way to live effectively is to rob the grave yard of what God has deposited in us for the benefits of mankind. We must fill the earth with the glory of His purpose for our lives as the waters cover the sea.

Habakkuk 2:14;

For the time will come when all the earth will be filled, as the waters fill the sea, with an awareness of the glory of the LORD. (NLT)

In this chapter, I will be showing with practical examples the glory of purpose discovered and fulfilled. As a matter of fact, God's grand design is that a time will come when all of His children will fill the earth with the glory He has ordained for us before the foundation of the world. That glory is found in the discovery and fulfillment of His purpose for our lives.

In the gospel of John chapter 17, verse 4 and 5, Jesus prayed thus; I have shown your glory on earth; I have finished the work you gave me to do.

Father! Give me glory in your presence now, the same glory I had with you before the world was made. (TEV)

This means our obedience to discovering and fulfilling God's original intention for us is the major way to bring glory to His name on earth as revealed through Jesus' prayer above.

In other words, you have a prepared glory with God long before you were sent to the earth. And your God given purpose is the container in which your glory was packaged from heaven. As you discover and pursue that divine purpose, that preordained glory will begin to see the light of day gradually on earth. And by the time you come to the full completion of the assignment of your God given purpose on earth, the fullness of that glory will fill the earth as the waters cover the sea.

Everyone and everything on earth is created with distinct and unique glory which can only be revealed through divine purpose. That is why purpose is not always the same. Just as the purpose of Mr. A is not the same as that of Mr. B, in the same way the purpose of Microphone is different from that of Saxophone, even though they have similar name.

1 Corinthians 15:41;

There is one glory of the sun, another glory of the moon, and another glory of the stars; for one star differs from another star in glory. (NKJV)

According to that statement above, the glory of one man is not the same as the glory of another man. Everything differs in glory. We cannot always accomplish the same kinds of feats in life because our God given purposes differ and so also our glories differ.

Now, a very powerful truth about glory is that if a man lived for 120 or more years on earth and did not make any tangible impact based on the purpose of God for him before his death, he has died with his glory.

The question now is **"What is glory?"**

Glory means; The true nature of a thing; The true essence of a thing,

The full release of one's God given ability,

Also, glory can be seen as beauty, splendor, resplendent majesty and distinction.

Glory is what God has preordained a thing to manifest on earth before the world was created. In other words, a man's glory is embedded in the full release of what God has deposited in him long before he exists on earth.

Therefore, glory is found within the context of discovery and pursuit of divine purpose. When destiny is discovered and fulfilled, glory is released.

Please note that giving glory to God is not just in dancing and singing praise to him in church or at home. Glory is far more than that. For instance, if you give praise and dance to God from morning till evening everyday of the week of every month of the year all through your life and you do not discover and fulfill His divine purpose for creating you, you have not given glory to His name.

Now that may sound absurd to religious people. Well, this book is not about religion, rather is it about kingdom realities. In as much as singing praise and dance unto God is His command to us; it does not change the truth that, the only thing in your life that glorifies God is the fulfillment of His purpose for your life.

Glory is not an idea of an imaginary smoke with a cloud of glory as some used to describe it; rather, glory is the revelation of God's nature is His creation. It is the manifestation of the true essence of the work of His hands. The doing and completion of God given task by His creature on earth is the manifestation of His glory.

Let me illustrate my points about glory here. Take for instance a planted tree in a garden. Before it begins to bear fruits, the first stage is to bring forth a bud in the stem. That bud does not look significant at that stage. As a matter of fact, it looks ugly and unattractive to us. However, within that ugly, unattractive bud is the flower which will eventually become the fruit of the tree. If that bud is cut off at that stage, the beauty and splendor of that tree which is its flower will never see the light of day. And that flower which eventually becomes the fruit is the glory of that tree. Once it is cut off at the bud stage, it dies with its glory. We do not go to look for buds on a tree; rather, we go for the fruits. Therefore, the death of a bud is the death of the glory of the tree.

This same truth is applicable to man. God's desire is that no man should die in the bud stage of his life. He wants every man to deliver the glory He has deposited in him before the earth was. God's desire is that we release our true nature and essence to benefit mankind. And this can only be made real as we discover and fulfill His purpose for us.

You may look insignificant, unattractive and ugly like that bud on the tree in the garden, but within you is beauty, splendor and glory that will fill the earth as the waters covers the sea.

The whole world is waiting for the manifestation of the glory which you had with God before the world began. Your goal in life is to find your purpose and fulfill it so that you do not go the grave yard with the glory that God has preordained for you. Your glory is not the same as the glory of your friend, therefore, do not try to imitate him; rather, locate your own unique purpose because your glory is trapped within the context of your purpose.

You should not allow crave for wealth, position and fame blind your eyes to the discovery of God's purpose for your life. You must sit down to locate what you were created to do.

Ask yourself these very important questions;

"Is what I am doing now what I am created to do?"

"Am I in the centre of God's plan and purpose for my life?"

"Is my life bringing any glory to God?"

It is your personal responsibility to find answers to those questions.

Take a look at the glory of men that have filled the earth as the water covers the sea.

The great man John Wesley has filled the earth with his glory through his ministry that gave birth to the Methodist Church world wide. He is no more but his glory lives on.

Also, men like Smith Wigglesworth, E.W. Kenyon are men that filled the earth with their glory before they passed on to glory. The world is still benefiting from their powerful message of faith.

The glory of Kenneth E. Hagin has filled the world with his word of faith message that has brought salvation, healing, deliverance and prosperity to people all around the world. He has passed on to glory beyond, but his glory on earth lives on.

Also, Oral Robert, a man whose glory still lives on through his establishment of Oral Robert University and many other schools has filled the earth with his glory.

Arch Bishop Benson Idahosa of Nigerian filled the earth with his glory through Church of God Mission, Benson Idahosa University before his departure from the earth.

The great man, Dr. David Oyedepo has filled the earth with his message of faith and prosperity that has brought about the building of the largest church auditorium on earth with seating capacity of 50,000 people. Also, his mission has built two world class universities (Covenant University, Ota and Landmark University, Omu Aran both in Nigeria), including many primary and secondary schools in different African nations.

I cannot write about all the other great men in the kingdom, whose glory have filled the earth as the waters cover the sea.

However, in the science and technology world, men have filled the earth with their God given glory.

The glory of Michael Faraday is found in electricity and his other scientific inventions. That glory has filled the earth as the waters covers the sea.

The glory of Orville and Wilbur Wright, popularly known as The Wright brothers is found in the invention of a system of aerodynamic control that manipulated a flying machine's surfaces (Aircraft). Today, many people have improved upon that invention and their glory has filled the earth as the water covers the sea.

In this modern day, we have men like Bill Gates, whose glory is found in his Microsoft products which are being used world wide and providing business solutions.

There will not be enough room in this chapter if we continue to talk about other men whose glory has filled the earth as the waters covers the sea. However, I have taken the time to outline those discoveries of men so that you can learn from their experiences and be determined to discover and release you own glory.

Your own glory is what the world is waiting to see now. If all these great men died without releasing their individual glory, we will not know about them today. That is not the will of God for you. God has created you to be a celebrity on earth and it is only your discovered and pursued purpose that can make that happen.

Friend; make a choice not to go to the grave yard with your glory unreleased. My soul is really desirous to see you release everything that God has put in you for the benefit of mankind before your time on earth is over. We are in the season for the manifestation of the glory of God through His people.

Romans 8:18-19;

---

18. For I reckon that the sufferings of this present time are not worthy to be compared with the glory which shall be revealed in us.

19 For the earnest expectation of the creature waiteth for the manifestation of the sons of God.

Do not allow, your present challenges blind your eyes to the glory of God trapped in you which is meant to be revealed to the world. The whole world waits eagerly for that glory in you to be manifested. By the time you are through reading this book, you too will discover your purpose and be determined to release your glory to bless the world.

Please, note that all the men I have written about above were for sometime unknown and unfulfilled. Many of them do not amount to much by people's estimation, but when it was time for their glory to manifest, nothing could stop them. And I believe that because they made it in spite of their challenges according to their stories, you, too will make it.

That glory in you which was put there by God to bless the world will see the light of day and it will fill the earth as the water covers the sea. Your glory will not be aborted in Jesus name.

Chapter 5: DISCOVER YOUR GOD GIVEN PURPOSE

Responsibility is the price for greatness Winston Churchill Your destiny is not your decision, it is your discovery. Destiny anchors on discovery of purpose - David Oyedepo

In the school of destiny, everyone is responsible for the discovery and ultimate fulfillment of his God given purpose. What is not discovered cannot be delivered.

However, it should be noted that, discovery of purpose begins with an encounter with God. It is not enough to understand what purpose is, you must go a step further to discover your own God given purpose and learn all that are required for its fulfillment.

Bear in mind that the most important thing to God is when His products perform the functions for which He has made them. Your purpose is the function that God created you to perform on earth and it is your responsibility to fulfill that function.

You are born to this earth because something peculiar was established by God concerning you before time began, but it is your responsibility to discover it. If you do not find out what God has ordained for your life, you can as well forget about achieving greatness in life, because greatness is a product of discovery of purpose which culminates in fulfillment of destiny.

What you should bother about is the discovery and fulfillment of the purpose for which God has created you. Although, your job could be part of the process for the discovery of your purpose, it may not be the real thing that God made you for. But because working is part of God's program for man, you need to get busy doing something, only that what you are doing is expected to be in line with God's purpose for you so that you will not just waste your valuable time and efforts in a wrong engagement.

However, if you have taken the time to seek for your purpose and you have discovered it; your life job should be centered on the fulfillment of that purpose.

My question to you is; ***"Are you in the right, God-ordained business?"***

Your life's purpose is the right business, but the business you are into may not be your purpose in life. Life is not about doing a business, rather, it is about doing the right business which is the pursuit of your life's purpose.

Also, you must be sure that you do not just do your job right, but be sure that you do the right job. Doing your job very well is a good thing, but doing the right job is the best thing. Purpose is the right job to do in life, because God counts you faithful only when you do the thing for which He has created you.

Your effectiveness is determined by doing that one thing that God has created you for. It does not matter how many things you do in life, God is only interested in your doing that one thing He has made you for. What I mean is that every other thing you do must be an aid to help in fulfilling the one purpose you are born for.

I want to illustrate my point with this instance.

I sent for a gardener to trim all the flowers in my compound and I told him: **"TRIM THE FLOWER IN THE COMPOUND".** And we agreed on a certain amount as his wage for that assignment. Then I left for my office after giving him the assignment with all the tools to do his work.

However, my gardener went straight into my garage and washed all the cars. He did not trim the flowers as I instructed.

Later in the evening, I returned home to find all the cars washed very clean and neat, but the flowers were not trimmed as I expected.

Then I met him still working on cleaning the cars. Then he came to welcome me. I looked at him and looked at the flowers not trimmed, but saw all the cars washed.

What do you think should be my reaction towards this gardener?

Although, he had washed all the cars, he has left the purpose for which I am obligated to pay him unattended. There is no way I will pay him for washing the cars, because that was not the assignment given to him. I am expected to pay him for trimming the flowers as we agreed, which he never did.

It reminds me of what Peter Drucker said; ***"There is nothing so useless as doing efficiently that which should not be done at all."***

Then, I told him; ***"Thank you for washing the cars, but I am obligated to pay you for***

trimming the flowers. You have done a very good job, but not the right one. Since you did not trim the flowers, there is no pay for you". Then he left disappointed.

This is the exact way God reacts to man, His product who is doing many good things except the right thing, which is the purpose for which He was made.

Friend, if you fail to fulfill divine purpose, you will not receive any commendation from God at the end of your journey on earth, because His interest lies only in your fulfilling His purpose for which He gave you life.

Jesus, who is God incarnate, had a history of how He worked as a carpenter with His earthly father, Joseph for the first 30 years of His life.

Although His name Jesus, came by prophecy that, He will save the world from their sins (Matthew 1:21), it was when He clocked 30 years that He went into the synagogue as His custom was and there He discovered what God had ordained Him to do on earth (Luke 4:16-17)

Jesus opened the book of prophecy and discovered what was written about Him by prophet Isaiah in chapter 61:1-3 of his book. Once He found it, He declared to the people the reality of what He has discovered about Himself.

Luke 4:21;

And he began to say unto them, This day is this scripture fulfilled in your ears.

He discovered the purpose of God for His life, which has been written concerning Him before the foundation of the world. And according to the account of this experience in the book of Hebrews as revealed to Paul from the book of Psalms, what Jesus discovered is the WILL of God for Him.

Hebrews 10:7;

Then said I, Lo, I come (in the volume of the book it is written of me), to do thy will, O God.

The WILL of God is the PURPOSE of God. And if Jesus must get to the point where He has to discover it, you and I must get to that point in our individual lives when each one will be able to say ***"I have found my purpose in life"***.

Discovery of purpose is the foundation for any landmark event in life and when we do not pay solid attention to foundation, we may not get the result that we expect.

The Psalmist, David said in Psalm 11:3;

If the foundations be destroyed, what can the righteous do?

Therefore, I believe that there is need to lay the foundation very well before the building starts. The ultimate fulfillment of destiny can be compared to a finished building, whose foundation must first be well laid before any other thing is done in the building process.

You are a product of God, the Sole Manufacturer, He has determined your purpose, but it is your responsibility to discover and fulfill it by His help. Therefore, what are the proven ways of discovering divine purpose?

DIVINE INSIGHT

This can as well be called revelation. Revelation or divine insight is the ability to gain access to what God has concluded concerning man before the world began. There is what God has finished concerning every of His children before creation, and only He can reveal it to each one by divine insight.

As well be called revelation. Revelation or divine insight is the ability to gain access to what God has concluded concerning man before the world began. There is what God has finished concerning every of His children before creation, and only He can reveal it to each one by divine insight.

Deuteronomy 29:29;

The secret things belong unto the LORD our God: but those things which are revealed belong unto us and to our children for ever, that we may do all the words of this law.

God is ever ready to reveal His purpose for man to him. As a matter of fact, He is always revealing it from time to time, but only those who are sensitive can see it. I believe that on several occasion, God might have reveal certain things to you about your future, although, you might not have paid much attention to it, or you might not be sensitive enough to pick it. That revelation is your purpose in life.

Revelation is the seed of destiny. Most times, it is a tiny seed that has to be nurtured to maturity.

God reveals things about our future in different forms and according to our level of readiness to obey Him. Also, He relates with us based on our level of understanding which grows as we grow in the knowledge of Him through His Word.

HOW TO RECEIVE DIVINE INSIGHT

Dream

Divine insight can come in form of a dream. A dream is a picture of your future as painted by God.

Joseph is a very good example of this. God showed him a picture of his future as a leader and preserver of a generation.

Genesis 37:5-6, 9;

And Joseph dreamed a dream, and he told it his brethren: and they hated him yet the more.

And he said unto them, Hear, I pray you, this dream which I have dreamed:

And he dreamed yet another dream, and told it his brethren, and said, Behold, I have dreamed a dream more; and, behold, the sun and the moon and the eleven stars made obeisance to me.

The dream of Joseph is the revelation of his God ordained purpose on earth. I believe that, God's assessment of Joseph in understanding spiritual things is the reason why He showed him a dream about the future. Thank God that Joseph discovered his purpose by revelation through dream.

I am of the opinion that if Joseph was not sensitive enough, he might not even pay attention to that dream, because it did not appear as anything real or possible. And ultimately, he would not have become a fulfilled man as a great leader in a strange land, Egypt. Joseph was sensitive to divine dream as his way of fulfilling God's purpose in life.

This truth was corroborated by what Joseph told his brothers Genesis 50:20 when the dream had been fulfilled.

As for you, you thought evil against me, but God meant it for good, to bring about that many people should be kept alive, as they are this day. (AMP)

Joseph's dream was the revelation of his purpose of keeping many people alive in the time of famine as he noted in that statement.

What is the dream that God keeps showing you? Do you pay attention to it?

I am not talking about nightmares, which come when one is sleeping in the night. I am talking about a picture that God hangs in you heart about your future.

I want you to stop reading for a moment and reflect on the dreams that God has given you in the past. Pay attention to it now and meditate on it. That could be your purpose in life. The best way you can know this is to ask yourself a question about that dream "is this a positive, value adding and people oriented dream?" if your answer is yes, ask God what it means and He will show you more and make it more clearer to you. That is your life purpose. God will show you if you will ask Him (Jeremiah 33:3)

Vision

Revelation of your purpose can come in form of a vision. Vision is very similar to dream, because it also has to do with seeing the future. Vision actually means to see what is coming to happen in the future by spiritual insight. Vision is to have a prior knowledge of upcoming events as relating to man. You can discover your purpose through vision that God shows you by His Spirit.

However, to see vision, you must be very active spiritually. As a matter of fact, God communicates to us by His Spirit and we must be very sensitive spiritually before we can receive visions from God.

The difference between a dream and a vision is that you may not hear any voice in a dream; but most times, vision is communicated with a combination of pictures and voice speaking to you to explain the vision.

Apostle Paul, whom I referred to several times in the previous chapters, had that experience of discovering God's purpose by vision. He had lived a wild and meaningless life hitherto, but the mercy of God located him and purpose was revealed to him by a vision on his way to Damascus (Acts 9:3-6).

This encounter was the turning point in Paul's life, because discovery of purpose creates a turning point and a new beginning for man. Paul did not only see the future, he heard the voice of the One who had predestined him for that purpose which was to carry the Gospel to the gentile nations.

I know that God has a vision for your future, but it is your responsibility to see that future.

Divine insight or revelation has the Holy Spirit as the source. He is the principal access to revelation. That is why; anyone who is not Born Again may not be able to discover purpose, because until a man is Born Again, he cannot have the Holy Spirit at work in him. And The Holy Spirit is our master revelator. (John 16:13)

The Holy Spirit speaks to us and shows us the purpose of God for creating us. It is very important then to have a personal relationship with the person of the Holy Spirit, because without Him, we cannot access the purpose in the mind of God for creating us.

1 Corinthians 2:9-10;

But as it is written, Eye hath not seen, nor ear heard, neither have entered into the heart of man, the things which God hath prepared for them that love him.

But God hath revealed them unto us by his Spirit: for the Spirit searcheth all things, yea, the deep things of God.

God is in heaven and Jesus is there with Him seated at His right hand; but the Holy Spirit, the 3rd Person of the Godhead is on the earth with us as the custodian of kingdom affairs. That is why the great thing that God has in stock for us as related to our divine destiny can only be shown to us by the Holy Spirit. He is the only one that can search the deep things of God.

The Holy Spirit reveals to us by speaking to us what God has in mind as His purpose for us. (Acts 8:29, Acts 10:19). The Holy Spirit is always speaking the mind of God.

What have you heard from Him? I know that you have heard a lot of things from people, but have you heard about your purpose from the Holy Spirit?

The voice of the Spirit could come to you in form of a still small voice (1 Kgs 19:12). It could come from behind you. (Isaiah 30:21). It could come audibly. (Acts 8:29). Whichever way it comes, it is your responsibility to recognize it and obey it. That is God speaking to you your purpose in life.

Scriptural Illumination (Revelation)

Again, the Holy Spirit can reveal your purpose by scriptural illumination. This happens mostly when you are studying the Word of God, or while you are meditating on scriptures.

There are many instances of this in the bible where men discovered their individual purpose in life by divine illumination through the Spirit of God.

Samuel, as a boy living with a prophet discovered his destiny by the appearance of God through His word.

1 Samuel 3:21;

And the LORD appeared again in Shiloh: for the LORD revealed himself to Samuel in Shiloh by the word of the LORD.

Daniel is another example of a man with discovery of God's plan by divine illumination. He was reading the Word of God as recorded by Prophet Jeremiah and God by the Holy Spirit showed him things to come concerning his nation.

Daniel 9:2;

During the first year of his reign, I, Daniel, was studying the writings of the prophets. I learned from the word of the LORD, as recorded by Jeremiah the prophet, that Jerusalem must lie desolate for seventy years. (NLT)

The discovery came while he was studying the Word of God. Remember also that, Jesus was reading the Word in the temple and He discovered what was written about Him as I noted earlier on in this chapter. (Luke 4:16-21).

This is the work of the Holy Spirit. He is the revelator by illumination of the Word of God. As a matter of fact, the word of God is the inspiration of the Holy Spirit packaged in scriptures. So the Holy Spirit will always quicken the Word in our spirit to deliver divine purpose to us (Isaiah 34:16)

No wonder Jesus said that the Word is Spirit and life. (John 6:63)

I am in the ministry today by the grace of God through revelation by divine illumination.

In the year 2003, between December 29 and 31, I was waiting on the Lord in a fast and studying the Word. On the 3rd day, the Holy Spirit illuminated the Word of God in Isaiah 58:12 in my spirit. Then the light came suddenly and I rose up and screamed "I found it today". That verse of the scripture is what has formed the vision statement of my ministry today. The Holy Spirit delivered to me God's mandate for my life on that fateful day and since then, I have been running with the vision.

Another thing you need to know is that the Word of God is the acid test for whatever voice you might have heard. When you hear a voice, you must be able to ascertain whether it is the Holy Spirit or the voice of the stranger. The best way to test this is to prove the voice by the Word of God. Anything you hear that takes away your peace is not from God. The Holy Spirit will always speak peace (Psalm 85:8)

Inward Witness

The Holy Spirit can reveal your purpose to you by an inner or inward witness. In this case, you did not hear a voice, neither did you see any vision, but there is a witness bearing consciousness of the Spirit within you. Essentially, the primary way the Holy Spirit leads us it through this inner or inward witness. He can guide or lead you into your purpose by bearing witness with your spirit.

Romans 8:14-16;

For as many as are led by the Spirit of God, they are the sons of God.

For ye have not received the spirit of bondage again to fear; but ye have received the Spirit of adoption, whereby we cry, Abba, Father.

The Spirit itself beareth witness with our spirit, that we are the children of God:

Please note that this method is used by the Holy Spirit as He wills, most especially, when it comes to confirming a dream, vision and divine illumination. May be He gave you a vision of your future, but you have not taken any step in its pursuit, He will come gently to bear witness with your spirit in confirming that vision. All you need is to be sensitive to Him at all times.

Also, His witness could be to warn you on certain steps you are about to take. Paul experienced this witness of the Spirit when he was determined to go to Jerusalem.

Acts 20:22-23;

And now, behold, I go bound in the spirit unto Jerusalem, not knowing the things that shall befall me there:

Save that the Holy Ghost witnesseth in every city, saying that bonds and afflictions abide me.

There was a very strong witness of the Holy Spirit about what was waiting for Paul at Jerusalem. That was why it was not a surprise to him when it happened as the Holy Spirit had earlier witnessed.

Prophetic Encounter

Prophets are agent of discovery and fulfillment of destiny. God has put prophets in the body of Christ to help people in locating the path God has ordained for them. Many lives and destinies are tied to certain prophetic ministries.

Prophets are ministry gifts to help men locate God's purpose in life. We have many examples in the Old Testament.

Saul located the throne through the ministry of Prophet Samuel. (1 Samuel 9:15-17). King David as well. (1 Samuel 16:10-13). Elisha fulfilled destiny through his connection to his prophet, Elijah. (2 Kings 2:1-15)

King Uzziah is another very good example of someone who received divine help through the ministry of a prophet. As long as he was operating with the revelation of Zechariah, his prophet, God prospered him. When he turned his back in pride from the instruction of his prophet, everything crashed for him. (2 Chronicles 26:1-15)

Prophets are carriers of divine insight into the ways of God. They are blessings to the body of Christ. They are not only spiritual fathers, but covenant fathers as ordained by God (Ephesians 4:11-13).

Divine perfection and fulfillment of destinies are tied to the prophetic ministry. We should not play down on this divine ordination. Seeking a prophetic covering is a biblical wisdom for the fulfillment of destiny.

I can say this with all sense of humility as a son of the prophet. My life and destiny is a product of my son-father relationship with my prophet, Dr. David Oyedepo. Having served with him for many years, God has given shape to my life and ministry.

However, care must be taken not to fall into the hand of fake prophets who are all around us. The fact that we have genuine prophet is a proof that there are fake ones.

Also, prophets are used by the Holy Spirit to confirm to us the mind of God for us. And we must prove whatever we hear by the Word of God and by checking the kinds of testimonies in the life of the prophet we follow. Someone who claims to be a prophet and instructs you to do things against the known Will of God is not a genuine prophet, you need to check it. The bible instructs us to prove all things (1 Thessalonians 5:21)

Prophetic instructions from genuine prophets are to be taken as the word of God, because they receive from the Holy Spirit and deliver it to us.

Therefore, we need the spirit of meekness to be able to follow the prophets that God sent to us. Our future is tied to the revelation of the Holy Spirit given to them for us. Take advantage of the prophetic ministry for the fulfillment of your destiny.

However, it should be noted that in all of the ways by which God reveals His plans and purpose to us by the Holy Spirit, it is done in phases. It is always precept upon precept, line upon line, a little here a little there. He does not show us everything about our destiny all at once (Isaiah 28:10).

God in His infinite wisdom, demands obedience to whatever He showed us, before He will show us the next one. He has ordained that we walk with Him by faith. That is why, He does not reveal His entire plan and purpose to us at once. From time to time as we obey Him, we are given access into a glimpse of the big picture of God for us. He unfolds His programs for us step by step as we go along with Him by faith.

Also, it is important for you to know that asking God in prayers to reveal His purpose to you is part of the process. Most times, God demands that we seek Him with all our heart for the revelation of His purpose.

He told Jeremiah in the first chapter Jeremiah 1:5;

Before I formed you in the womb I knew [and] approved of you [as My chosen instrument], and before you were born I separated and set you apart, consecrating you; [and] I appointed you as a prophet to the nations. (AMP)

Again, God told him in the 29th chapter that there is a great plan in His agenda for him, but there is an instruction that go along with that revelation. That instruction is that there is a need to seek the face of God in prayer for the revelation of the great plan that He has for him. (Jeremiah 29:11-13)

God is willing and ready when we obey Him by seeking and asking Him to show us His purpose for creating us.

CHECK YOUR DESIGN

Another major way by which you can discover your life purpose is to locate your design. God spent qualitative time in molding your frame after He has determined your purpose. Therefore, He designed and molded you according to the purpose and the assignment He has for you on earth. (Psalm 139:13-16).

All the parts of your soul and body were fashioned by God to fit to your purpose. Your thinking ability, body complexion, height, weight, stature etc. were all put into consideration by God when He manufactured you in His heavenly factory. And He carefully molded your frame to conform to your purpose.

For instance, many people who are making waves in sports industry today are there because they discovered that they were designed specifically by God for the kind of sport they are into. There are many footballers, wrestlers, basketball players, athletes who are fulfilling purpose as they use their discovered design.

God designed the leg of a footballer to play football, many basketball players are tall as designed by God, and many weight lifters have very strong muscles fitted for their assignment as designed by God.

Although, they work very hard in developing their design in order to match up with their discovered purpose. Many of them spend hours everyday to train up their body system and as they keep training, they keep improving until that discovered design brought them up to the top in their careers.

YOUR GIFTS AND TALENTS

Also, God put in you certain talents and gifts because of the kind of assignment He has for you on earth. The talents and gifts in you are peculiar as a result of the peculiarity of your purpose. You need to pay attention to this by discovering the endowments of God in you. Your talents and gifts are divine endowments which are pointers to the discovery of your purpose in life.

Few years ago, I read this statement made by one wise man; "When God created you, He gave you certain gifts and talents to accomplish something He wanted. Your strongest desire, talents and opportunities reveal God's calling and dream for your life."

It is imperative for you to understand that there is no one created by God without certain endowment required to fulfill His purpose in life.

In the parable of Jesus as recorded by Matthew in chapter 25, verses 14 and 15;

For the kingdom of heaven is as a man travelling into a far country, who called his own servants, and delivered unto them his goods.

And unto one he gave five talents, to another two, and to another one; to every man according to his several ability; and straightway took his journey.

Everyone was given something according the ability and capacity of each one. There is no one on earth without something given him by God to make him fulfill destiny.

In a similar instance, every one that was given the gifts were instructed to use it for a purpose as recorded in

Luke 19:12-13;

Therefore He said: "A certain nobleman went into a far country to receive for himself a kingdom and to return.

So he called ten of his servants, delivered to them ten minas, and said to them, 'Do business till I come.' (NKJV)

There is what to do with the gifts of God in you. He did not put the gift there for the sake of it, but for the fulfillment of your purpose as you 'do business with it'

The word 'business' in that passage means; to get busy using the gifts and talents of God in you for profitability. One of the major objectives of business is profit; therefore the gift of God in you is to do business for profit and that profit is the fulfillment of God's purpose for creating you.

That which God has given you is all you need to become a person of influence on earth. Your gift is a blessing to your world, because it makes you stand out in life as you discover it and work on it. The gifts and talents of God put in you will create opportunities for your fulfillment of destiny Proverbs 18:16).

When God gives anything to a man, it is for the purpose of fulfilling that man's purpose. And He does not withdraw it from man, even if the man refuses to acknowledge and put it to use (Romans 11:29).

That speaking ability, writing gifts, teaching talents, creative thinking ability, singing gift etc. in man are put there by God for a purpose and the purpose is for the fulfillment of divine purpose.

There are many who are making waves today all over the world and all they did was to leverage on the gifts and talents of God in them. Many of them did not have any divine insight, they just looked inward to the gift of God in them and developed it and put the gifts to use. They are fulfilling God's purpose for creating them using their discovered design, gifts and talents.

In case you are reading this book now and you have not received any form of divine insight, then look inward to your gifts and talents. They are pointers to your purpose in life. Your main work is to discover that gift and develop it. God gave them to man in a raw state, but it is man's responsibility to refine and develop it by reason of constant use and training. When it is used, it brings profit and when it is not used, it remains dormant in you.

Discover and use your gifts and talents; they have the ability of creating a great future of fulfilled destiny for you.

WHAT ARE YOUR EXPERIENCES?

Another way by which you can discover your purpose is to check the experiences and challenges in your life.

God in His infinite wisdom uses these to bring man into the fulfillment of His purpose in life. Although this may not be the case for all men, but certain people fall into this category as designed by God. Sometimes, God allows man to go through some form of challenges and adversities in order to reveal His future plan and assignment for him.

That is why I know that challenges and some negative experiences are designed by God to achieve His purpose for some people as I have discovered by research.

David as a boy was neglected in his father's farm among the sheep. He had no friends or acquaintances at that very young age. He was busy, taking care of his father's sheep. And he remained faithful to his work as a shepherd boy.

David perhaps did not know what God had in mind for him, neither are we told that he had a dream of becoming a ruler, like Joseph.

God took him through that experience in order to prepare him for the assignment of leadership as a king in Israel. (1 Samuel 16:11-13)

When David was still with the sheep in the wilderness, God gave him two experiences of defending the sheep by killing a lion and a bear that came to attack them. He did not know why.

And a time came when Israel was besieged by the Philistines led by the giant, Goliath; no one was able to confront this giant, except David. He was able to do this because he remembered how God gave him victory over the lion and the bear in the wilderness. He leveraged on those experiences and he was able to defend Israel by killing Goliath the way he killed the lion and the bear (1 Samuel 17:32-37).

It was not a surprise to anyone that David became one of the greatest Kings in Israel. God took him to the throne by taking him through challenges and different experiences of life.

There are many other examples of this kind in the Bible. For instance, Moses who delivered Israel from Egypt had a similar experience. (Exodus 2:11-14, Exodus 3:1-10)

Again, Gideon was another example of this principle of discovery of divine purpose. He was located for leadership in the midst of challenges and trials. (Judges 6:11-14)

Friend, what are your experiences and challenges in life? Pay attention to them with a positive mentality, they are pointers to your God given purpose in life. There is something God wants you to see in the midst of those challenges. There is a problem that God wants to bring solution to through you and that could be the same kind of experience you are having right now. Do not see it as a negative issue; there is a positive situation coming out of it. All you need is to be spiritually sensitive and you will see the good aspect of it.

It was Washington Irving that said; **"It is interesting to notice how some minds seem almost to create themselves, springing up under every disadvantage, and working their solitary but irresistible way through a thousand obstacles."**

In a very close manner, Arthur Golden puts it this way; **"Adversity is like a strong wind. It tears away from us all but the things that cannot be torn, so that we see ourselves as we really are."**

You too can walk your way to God's purpose for your life through those challenges you are faced with right now. Open up your heart to see the good aspect of it and turn your setbacks into a setup for a powerful come back.

Your gifts and talents can be trained through adversity and challenges that you face in life. Just commit yourself to the positive aspect. God will use those adversities and obstacles to bring you into the maturity needed to fulfill your purpose.

2 Corinthians 4:17;

For our light, momentary affliction (this slight distress of the passing hour) is ever more and more abundantly preparing and producing and achieving for us an everlasting weight of glory [beyond all measure, excessively surpassing all comparisons and all calculations, a vast and transcendent glory and blessedness never to cease!] (AMP)

The weight of glory is the full release of your purpose, but the experiences of adversity and obstacles helps in bringing it forth.

Adversity is the breeding ground for miracles. Most of the time, the greatest fire of accomplishments burns from the ashes of defeat. Your miracle fulfillment can come from your challenges and experiences. Make the most of them.

CHECK YOUR PASSION

Your passion is another divine endowment that God has put in you as a pointer to your purpose in life. Passion is that inward drive and strong desire to accomplish something outstanding. It is the inner power possessed by an individual to solve a particular problem. Your purpose in life is a problem you are born to solve. And you may not receive any divine insight about this, but there is something on the inside that is driving you to see a problem solved. That is your passion.

It is your passion that reveals what you carry as your purpose. Without that inner drive, you cannot fulfill the purpose. When you discover you passion, you have discovered you assignment in life. Also, it is passion that keeps you going in the face of adversity. It is passion that makes you cry from the inside to see a situation changed.

A strong passion for any object will ensure success, for the desire of the end will point out the means. That desire of the end is your purpose, but it takes passion to work it out. You will not run after what you are not passionate about. Purpose helps you develop a strong passion for actualizing your destiny. Passion is when you have found something to die for, not just what to live for. Just like the hardware needs software to function, in the same way purpose needs passion to be activated to fulfillment.

Dr. John C. Maxwell said; ***"Passion is the difference-maker. Without passion we stop dreaming and settle for survival. We relinquish heartfelt vision in exchange for security and comfort."***

It is passion that gives you a mentality of one who is on a mission to servicing the needs of the people. And destiny fulfillment anchors on service.

There is this account about Nehemiah in the bible. He did not receive any revelation about his purpose, but with a passion to solve problem for his people, he fulfilled a divine purpose. Nehemiah took it upon himself to see the rebuilding of the broken down wall of Jerusalem. He moved with passion and it was done. That experience made him ascend the throne of leadership as a governor in Judah. (See Nehemiah chapter 1-5)

The founder of Virgin Empire, Richard Branson once said; ***"Ideally, since 80 percent of your life is spent working, you should start your business around something that is a passion of yours."***

In other words, your purpose and assignment in life is found in your passion. Check your passion and you will discover your purpose.

It is your passion is what gives you your own portion in your nation. You are either running with a vision, burning with a passion or trading with a gift. There is no reason that is strong enough for any man not to fulfill his destiny in life. You will get to the ultimate of God for your life as you pay full attention to the truth I have shared in this chapter.

As you move to the next chapter, please understand, that the question of purpose must be answered by every man before destiny can be fulfilled. This chapter has given you the answer; therefore, go for your own discovery now.

Chapter 6: PERSONAL PREPARATION DIMENSION

God will take whatever time is needed to develop and train you before He brings to pass what He has spoken to your heart. - Kenneth E. Hagin

If you wish to achieve worthwhile things in your personal and career life, you must become a worthwhile person in your own self-development. - Brian Tracy

No man ever reached to excellence in any one art or profession without having passed

through the slow and painful process of study and preparation. - Horace Mann

It is the preparation involved in your purpose that determines the delivery and ultimate fulfillment of that purpose in life. If you desire to fulfill your purpose, you must engage in extraordinary preparation.

God, the author of purpose is very keen about how we respond to His program for the fulfillment of His purpose for us. The reason for this is that, He has something great to achieve on earth through us by giving us that purpose. He has designed that man, His image and exact representation will be the one to carry out His program on earth. That was the reason why at creation, He gave man the mandate:

...have dominion over the fish of the sea, and over the fowl of the air, and over the cattle, and over all the earth, and over every creeping thing that creepeth upon the earth. (Genesis 1:26)

Dominion over ALL THE EARTH has been given to man and that can only happen when man discovers his purpose on earth. So God expects nothing less than fulfillment of purpose from man.

Therefore, He commands us to:

Prepare thy work without, and make it fit for thyself in the field; and afterwards build thine house (Proverbs 24:27),

Prepare ye the way of the LORD, make straight in the desert a highway for our God. (Isaiah 40:3),

Prepare ye the way of the people; cast up, cast up the highway; gather out the stones; lift up a standard for the people. (Isaiah 62:10),

Be thou prepared, and prepare for thyself, thou, and all thy company that are assembled unto thee, and be thou a guard unto them. (Ezekiel 38:7)

Prepared, and prepare for thyself, thou, and all thy company that are assembled unto

thee, and be thou a guard unto them. (Ezekiel 38:7)

Prepare the way before me: and the Lord, whom ye seek, shall suddenly come to his temple, even the messenger of the covenant, whom ye delight in: behold, he shall come, saith the LORD of hosts. (Malachi 3:1)

There is power in preparation as it leads to outstanding accomplishment.

Personal Preparation is a major factor for personal fulfillment. Every outstanding accomplishment in life has its root in outstanding preparation. And preparation for the fulfillment of destiny is the responsibility of the individual who desires fulfillment.

WHAT IS PREPARATION?

According to Encarta Dictionary, preparation means:

The works of planning involved in making something or somebody ready,

Putting something together in advance,

Something done in advance in order to be ready for a future event,

A state of readiness.

Preparation is the act of planning by way of putting something together or getting something or someone set in advance in order to be ready for a future event.

The fulfillment of your purpose is a future event because, God has ordained that every of His program for man will always speak at the end (Habakkuk 2:1-3). In other words, what you have discovered as your purpose in life will be accomplished at a future time set by God, but determined by your readiness to see it accomplished.

The key to get to that future time is preparation. The deeper your preparation, the faster and easier you see your purpose accomplished.

It was recorded concerning a young king named Jotham in the book of 2 Chronicles 27:6;

So Jotham became mighty, because he prepared his ways before the LORD his God.

The outstanding feat in the life of Jotham was a product of his preparation. If your name must enter life's book of success and fulfillment of purpose, you must engage in qualitative preparation for the fulfillment of that God given purpose.

You cannot leave your purpose to chance fulfillment, with a mentality of 'God will do it'. What God will do is to help you as you go on. But the preparation aspect is major before you can secure His help.

That qualitative preparation is described as self-education by Jim Rohn, when he said; *"Formal education will make you a living; self-education will make you a fortune"*

Recently, I was searching my files for a document and I found one of my study notes in 2003, where I wrote the following;

"Until you prepare for life, you are not prepared to live. The quality of your life is a product of the quality of your preparations". (10th March, 2003)

Every great building such as skyscrapers requires a high level of preparation as compared with a bungalow. A lot of time is spent and more resources are put into preparation for building a skyscraper because of its height and the number of floors it has.

Your level of accomplishment is limited by the level of your preparation, because God will not make happen for you what you are not prepared for.

Your purpose in life is a kind of building as I noted in the previous chapter, and it requires adequate preparation before you begin. Also, your preparation will depend on what kind of building your purpose is likened to. As I noted above, preparation for a bungalow is not as tasking as preparation for a skyscraper.

If a natural building requires such high level preparation, how much more a spiritual assignment which is God's purpose for you?

No one will do the preparation for you, because, your purpose is peculiar to you. Although, it is for the fulfillment of God's master plan, it is not the same as the purpose of another person. That is why preparation must be personal in the same way discovery of purpose is personal.

Proverbs 16:1;

The preparations of the heart in man, and the answer of the tongue, is from the LORD.

Proverbs 16:9;

A man's mind plans (prepares) his way, but the Lord directs his steps and makes them sure. (AMP)

Preparation is a personal responsibility of each man desiring to fulfill divine purpose.

DIFFERENT LEVELS OF PREPARATION

Personal preparation has different dimensions and some of the dimensions will be discussed in this segment.

Spiritual Preparation

This is the foundational preparation dimension. It is one of the most fundamental aspects in our bid to fulfill God's purpose.

The spiritual life controls every other aspects of life. There is no way any man can fulfill divine purpose without submitting to the laws of God who is the author of that purpose. No matter what you have discovered as your life assignment, you need to prepare spiritually before you begin the pursuit.

Spiritual preparation means seeking the face of God in order to secure His help in fulfilling His purpose for us.

However, Spiritual preparation has different dimensions to it which include:

Consistent Prayers

Prayer is the most authentic communication channel between God and man. It is not enough to discover God's purpose for us; we need to receive the necessary instructions needed to carry out the tasks involved in fulfilling the purpose.

Also, we need spiritual empowerment that will shield us from all satanic assault that may stand in our ways of fulfilling that discovered purpose. And without a consistent prayer life, divine purpose cannot be accomplished.

Your purpose is from God; therefore, the fulfillment will have to be by His help. And it is through constant prayer that we can secure the help of God required for the successful pursuit of our purpose in life.

On the importance of prayer, Dr. Myles Munroe shared this view; ***"Prayer is important because it is our means of constantly granting God permission to interfere in the affairs of men on earth. God can do anything, but because He has given us the license, He can release on the earth only what we allow."***

God will only respond to the prayers of His people on earth because He has given us the dominion over the earth. And in order to fulfill the dominion mandate of fulfilling His purpose for us; we need to call unto Him in prayers from time to time to secure His grace.

I believe in how Dr. Mike Murdock puts it, when he said; ***"One hour with God daily could easily reveal to you the fatal flaws in your most carefully laid plans. He who succeeds in prayer succeeds."***

Prayer is the master key to the throne of God where we can obtain the grace and help needed to fulfill destiny. (Hebrew 4:16)

Also, one major way to maintain a strong spiritual life full of the Holy Spirit is to maintain a close fellowship with God through prayer as we seek His face daily.

Luke 18:1;

And he spake a parable unto them to this end, that men ought always to pray, and not to faint.

Prayer must be a part of your life if you desire to fulfill purpose. However, one major aspects of prayer that we need to learn is, praying in the Holy Spirit. This is also known as praying in tongue.

This is the best way to pray the plan and purpose of God in advance as we prepare to fulfill destiny. As I noted earlier that the purpose of God is His Will and Plan and when we pray in the Spirit, we are praying according to His Will, Plan or Purpose for our lives.

Romans 8:26-27;

Likewise the Spirit also helpeth our infirmities: for we know not what we should pray for as we ought: but the Spirit itself maketh intercession for us with groanings which cannot be uttered.

And he that searcheth the hearts knoweth what is the mind of the Spirit, because He maketh intercession for the saints according to the will of God.

Praying in the Holy Ghost is praying the Will, Plan or Purpose of God into reality. Also, it helps in building up the faith you need to carry out God's plan and purpose for your life (Jude 20)

Without faith, you cannot commit God for His help, as it is only with faith that you can please God. (Hebrews 11:6)

Therefore, as you seek God for the fulfillment of His purpose for your life, commit to praying in the Spirit from time to time. And in case you are not baptized in the Holy Spirit, seek to be baptized, because without it, you will not be able to fully deliver your divine mandate on earth.

Also, fasting should be added to prayers from time to time in order to accelerate spiritual growth as prompted by the Holy Spirit.

Matthew 17:21;

Howbeit this kind goeth not out but by prayer and fasting.

eit this kind goeth not out but by prayer and fasting.

Fasting added to prayer will help in dislodging all satanic plots in your way of fulfillment. (Isaiah 58:6-7)

Fasting will also grant you access to fresh light from God as you seek His face. It will help your spirit man to be more active than your flesh and when you are spiritually active, you are able to pick divine signals and instructions needed for the fulfillment of your purpose.

Also, following the plan and purpose of God for your life is equal to obedience to His Will and His promise of answers to your prayers will be delivered to you as you do His Will which includes thanksgiving and praise. (Hebrews 10:36)

Thanksgiving and praise grant you access to fresh anointing that will empower you against enemies of your fulfillment. When you are thanking God in prayers, you are being empowered with new anointing. (Psalm 92:1-2, 10)

The divine strength that we need to fulfill destiny will also be delivered through the channel of prayer and fasting with thanksgiving and praise (Isaiah 40:31)

This is what Jesus did when He was about to begin the full pursuit of His purpose in life. He went to the wilderness and fasted for forty days. (Matthew 4:1-2, Mark 1:13, Luke 4:1-2)

He did not stop at that, but as He was in the pursuit of His purpose, He always took time out to seek God's face in prayer alone as recorded in Mark 1:35

And in the morning, rising up a great while before day, he went out, and departed into a solitary place, and there prayed.

If Jesus needed to pray to seek God's face, you and I need to follow in His steps if we desire to fulfill God's purpose for our lives. God will never give you a dream or purpose or assignment that does not require Him to accomplish. And since your purpose is given by God, you will always need His constant and continuous intervention in your bid to accomplish the purpose. Therefore, keep pushing in prayer as you prepare for your destiny.

Committed Word study

The Word of God is the source of faith and faith is required in fulfilling divine purpose. The knowledge of the Word of God is very essential for our spiritual growth and that knowledge can be gained through a commitment to daily Word study.

Daniel 11:32;

...but the people that do know their God shall be strong, and do exploits.

Romans 10:17;

So then faith cometh by hearing, and hearing by the word of God.

The more of God's knowledge you have access to the more prepared you are to fulfill your purpose. The Word of God grants you access to divine wisdom which is the most important key in fulfilling God's purpose (Proverbs 4:7)

Wisdom is defined as the correct application of knowledge. It is the effective utilization of the knowledge acquired from the Word of God. The Word of God makes wise. Paul noted this about His ministry son, Timothy in 2 Timothy 3:15;

And that from a child thou hast known the holy scriptures, which are able to make thee wise unto salvation through faith which is in Christ Jesus.

When we give attention to the Word of God as we study it constantly, we release our natural wisdom for divine wisdom which is a major key to fulfilling our destiny. Divine wisdom produces divine strength and divine strength produces great exploits. And that wisdom is the one from above which we encounter from the Word of God. (Matthew 13:54, Proverbs 24:5, Daniel 11:32)

Also, you can accelerate you understanding of the Word of God by committing yourself to learning from spiritual leaders through their teaching tapes and books. This is a very important aspect of spiritual growth, because, you may not understand certain truths in the Bible on your own. God has put men in the body of Christ who are light bearers and we can gain access to greater light from God's Word, by hearing their teaching in tapes or reading their books.

Daniel who is a man of great exploits, gained understanding into the purpose of God by reading the book of Jeremiah. (Daniel 9:2)

Paul became a man of strange level of spiritual insight by his commitment to the reading of books. (2 Timothy 4:13, 1 Timothy 4:13-15)

The tapes and books of these men are released in order to help our faith. Most times, their materials contain the story of how they accomplish God's purpose which, when we hear or read about, we develop their kind of faith to fulfill our own destiny.

Reading must become a part of your life if you must fulfill your purpose on earth, because through reading you gain access to knowledge and understanding required for accomplishment.

In his book, Following God's Plan For Your Life, the great man of faith, Kenneth E. Hagin said; ***"Days of preparation are never lost time. There may be important lessons or truth that you still need to learn in order to successfully fulfill God's plan for you. And it takes time to prepare and establish yourself in God's Word. However, going through a time of preparation is not always easy, for sometimes there is a price to be paid. From your perspective, your preparation time might not always be comfortable because you might have to die to your own desires*** *and your timing as you allow God to prepare you."*

Your preparation will take time and you need to take the time to prepare spiritually as you commit to consistent prayer and committed Word study on a daily basis.

Also, time should be set aside specially to seek God's face in preparation for the next level of God's assignment for you.

Lay Aside Every Weight And Sin

Pursuing your purpose in life is running a spiritual race that God has set before you. Just like no athlete can successfully run a race with his overcoat on, in the same way, you cannot run your spiritual race, which is your purpose with any kind of weight and sin. Before you begin the pursuit of your discovered purpose in life, it is your responsibility to lay aside the weight and sin which will definitely hinder you from successful pursuit.

Hebrews 12:1;

Wherefore seeing we also are compassed about with so great a cloud of witnesses, let us lay aside every weight, and the sin which doth so easily beset us, and let us run with patience the race that is set before us.

Running your race in life without laying aside the weight and sin will slow you down, in the same way an overcoat will slow an athlete down in running an Olympic race.

Therefore, you owe God and yourself the responsibility of stripping off anything that slows you down or holds you back, and especially those sins that wrap themselves so tightly around your feet and trip you up; as The Living Bible renders Hebrews 12:1.

Friend, sin will slow you down, it will keep tripping you up, and it can prevent you from running your race successfully as you pursue your purpose. If you run the race half way before you start to lay those things aside, you will have trouble in continuing and finishing the race.

What are those weights or sin in your own life? Those wrong motives, carnal inclinations, desires of the flesh and selfish ambitions. Or is it pride, fear, spiritual slothfulness double-mindedness and the likes?

Another aspect of laying aside the weight and sin is to be careful not to become too entangled with legitimate affairs of life. These are things that may be good in themselves, but are not in line with what God has created you to do in life. Although there are many things in life that are not necessarily wrong, but they will slow you down in the pursuit of your peculiar purpose.

God will not do it for you, it is your responsibility, but the help of God is available for you to do it if you're a willing. That is why you cannot succeed without prayer. As you pray consistently, God will send you help to get it done. All He wants is your willingness to be fully prepared for His purpose for you.

Preparation in Specialized Training

Training is a major virtue for preparation, because, it enables you to achieve effectiveness in your assignment.

Training can be defined as the act of learning specified skill by practice. Also, it means, the process of attaining physical efficiency by exercise.

In other word, you will come to a point of achieving effectiveness and efficiency in the tasks involved in your purpose as you engage in the process of acquiring the specified Skill, Knowledge, Ability that leads to Competence in your delivery.

Henry Ford once said; ***"If money is your hope for independence you will never have it. The only real security that a man will have in this world is a reserve of knowledge, experience, and ability."***

For instance, if your discovered purpose is to establish a business, having done your necessary research on what the business entails, you need to proceed to the level of acquiring the Skill, Knowledge, Ability and Competence required to accomplish that purpose. Do not just start investing into that business without first acquiring the necessary skills.

There is no celebrated Medical Doctor who did not spend about six or seven years in school, acquiring the skill, knowledge, ability and competence required. He does not stop there, after the seven years in school; he goes for another dimension of training as he prepares himself to begin the medical practice. And from time to time, he engages in other levels of training as he advances in his practice.

Peter Drucker, the world renowned Management expert once said; *"We now accept the fact that learning is a lifelong process of keeping*

abreast of change. And the most pressing task is to teach people how to learn."

Jesus spent thirty years in preparation for the assignment which He spent only three and half years to accomplish. When He was twelve years old, He went into the temple to learn from the religious doctors and lawyers of His day. This is because; He needed to know about the state of things in the community where He would later emerge as a star to fulfill His purpose. When His earthly parents found Him after a three-day seminar He was attending, he told them that He was training on how to carry out His Father's business (purpose) on earth. It was later recorded about Him in the same chapter how He increased in wisdom which is largely a result of the training He engaged in earlier on. (Luke 2:46-52)

Also, it was recorded about Paul how he went into a personal preparation for about 3 years in Arabia after he was called into the ministry. He separated himself into a solitary place to learn and acquire the necessary Skill, Knowledge, Ability and Competence required to fulfill his discovered purpose. (Galatians 1:15-18)

No wonder Paul accomplished great things and made maximum impact in his assignment, to which Peter testified about the strange order of insight and wisdom he was given by God as he subjected himself to a long period of preparation. (2 Peter 3:15-16.)

Abraham, the Great, understood the place of training in the successful pursuit of any given assignment. When they captured Lot, his brother, Abraham went to rescue him with his trained servants.

In other words, he had prepared for war in the time of peace by training his servants.

Genesis 14:14;

And when Abram heard that his brother was taken captive, he armed his trained servants, born in his own house, three hundred and eighteen, and pursued them unto Dan.

Abraham returned from that war and brought back home all that the enemy had stolen. This was a result of preparation by training.

Training is the backbone of an army. There is no successful soldier who has not subjected himself to various forms of training over the years in the pursuit of his military career.

David is another example. He was able to kill Goliath by virtue of the training that God used to prepare him. God taught him how to kill a lion and a bear in order to prepare him for the killing of Goliath. (1 Samuel 17:32-37)

Psalm 18:34;

He teacheth my hands to war, so that a bow of steel is broken by mine arms.

The training you engage in is a part of the keys needed to carry out your divine purpose which is the Father's business for you on earth.

Champions are not made in the ring, rather, they are made in the secret place of preparation; they are only recognized as champions in the ring.

Your training will require reading of all books and materials that will help you acquire the Skill, Knowledge, Ability and Competence needed for the ultimate fulfillment of your purpose. You will need to engage in specific research relating to your assignment. You will need to take certain classes of lectures from time to time.

In the corporate business world, organizations invest multimillion dollars every year on Training, Research and Development. This is for the purpose of effective accomplishment of their goals and objectives in delivering quality products and services in order to maximize profit.

God is saying to you; ***"My son prepare, prepare, prepare for your future. It is the key to your ultimate fulfillment."***

Take the time to prepare yourself by training before you begin and as you go on in your pursuit, commit yourself to more training required to improve on your previous success.

Dr. David Oyedepo once said; Preparation is the mother of manifestation. What you do not prepare for, you cannot experience.

Personal preparation does not have an end. It must be continuous as you move from one phase of your purpose to another phase. Purpose is not fulfilled all at once, because God will not show you all that you need to do at once. As you grow in your pursuit, you must keep growing in your preparation everyday. Spiritual preparation and specialized training are part of God's agenda for your fulfillment. Therefore, take this with all seriousness.

Chapter 7: DILIGENCE OF PURPOSE

Learn how to grow out of yourself and into the world of others. Plant a shade tree under which you know you will never sit. Set some goals that may benefit your children or an orphanage or the employees of your company or future generations of your own city, fifty years from now. - Dennis Waitley

I believe life is constantly testing us for our level of commitment, and life's greatest rewards are reserved for those who demonstrate a never-ending commitment to

act until they achieve. This level of resolve can move mountains, but it must be constant and consistent. As simplistic as this may sound, it is still the common denominator separating those who live their dreams from those who live in regret. -
Anthony Robbins

The purpose that is not pursued cannot be accomplished. It is only the discovery that is pursued that can be recovered. There is no discovered purpose that has the capacity for self fulfillment unless it is pursued by man.

However, in this chapter, I will be dwelling on the importance of diligence, which is hard work in the pursuit of your purpose. You need to understand that, the dream you do not dare will die or it remains a daydream (fantasy).

By way of definition, diligence simply means persistent effort or hard-working efforts in doing something. It means industry, meticulousness and thoroughness in the pursuit of your purpose. Another word for diligence is hard-working.

It takes diligent pursuit to accomplish any given task in life. Your discovered purpose is your task in life as I have noted earlier and to accomplish it, you must pursue it with all diligence. It is a well known fact in the school of successful accomplishment that, if you are going to achieve any dream, you will have to work it out just like everybody who have achieved their dreams have done.

1 Corinthians 9:24-26;

Know ye not that they which run in a race run all, but one receiveth the prize? So run, that ye may obtain.

And every man that striveth for the mastery is temperate in all things. Now they do it to obtain a corruptible crown; but we an incorruptible.

I therefore so run, not as uncertainly; so fight I, not as one that beateth the air.

The amazing reality of life is that all runners in a race are candidates for the prize, but only one out of all that run gets the highest prize, because, every sport has it rule. It takes running according to the rules that qualify you for the prize. You cannot obtain until you run and even if you run, you are only qualified for the prize if you run according to the laid-down rules of the game.

In the world of sports, there are Gold, Silver and Bronze medals. The first three winners are given the medals according to their respective positions after the game. The truth is that they all ran in the race, but they ended up with different positions which determined the prize they are going home with.

It is imperative to know that, behind every thing moving, there is a mover. And only those who are making moves can cause waves in the race of life. Your purpose demands prompt and constant moves from you, if you desire its fulfillment. You will need to engage the spiritual, intellectual and physical rules to fulfill your purpose. And God has laid down those rules for us to run the race set before each of us with all diligence.

Diligence in this context means hard work in the right direction. It does not mean just working hard, but working hard on your discovered purpose; doing everything in your power as enabled by God to fulfill your purpose.

In other words, it is possible to be working hard and not be diligent. This is because; it is not enough to be working hard, your hard work must be in the direction of your discovered purpose. That is why, effectiveness is not measured by hard work only, rather, it is measured by diligence which is hard work directed to accomplishing a given task.

It takes a consistent daily pursuit to fulfill any divine purpose. What you do not work out cannot work out. There has to be a commitment to the various tasks involved in your assignment everyday until you see the reality of that purpose.

Philippians 2:12;

...work out your own salvation with fear and trembling

I like the way Paul described his diligence in his epistle to the church at Corinth as recorded in 1 Corinthians 15:10;

But by the grace of God I am what I am: and his grace which was bestowed upon me was not in vain; but I laboured more abundantly than they all: yet not I, but the grace of God which was with me.

Paul had an unusual encounter with divine purpose on his way to Damascus as recorded in Acts 9:1-10, and he rose up from that encounter to work it out by spiritual, mental and physical labour. He acknowledged the grace of God as being responsible for his exploits in ministry, but he immediately noted that he did not sit down with that grace to have taken him to that point without labour.

Paul gave his entire life to his discovered purpose by labouring fervently daily until the time of his departure from the earth. He labored abundantly and finished his assignment.

Proverbs 14:23;

In all labour there is profit: but the talk of the lips tendeth only to penury.

Profit in your assignment answers to your consistent labour. In this context, labour means diligence. It is not just working hard; it is working smart as you focus your efforts on your assignment in life.

It is common knowledge that there has to be labour before any child birth. And every labour to give birth comes with some degree of pain.

Isaiah 66:7-8;

Before she goes into labor, she gives birth; before the pains come upon her, she delivers a son.

Who has ever heard of such a thing? Who has ever seen such things? Can a country be born in a day or a nation be brought forth in a moment? Yet no sooner is Zion in labor than she gives birth to her children. (NIV)

Your discovered purpose is like a pregnancy of destiny in your belly. The delivery of every pregnancy requires the labour room. If you want to deliver the pregnancy of God in you which is your discovered purpose, you must submit yourself to the pain of labour in the labour room of diligence.

Just as the pregnant woman will be required to 'push' to deliver the baby, you must 'push' by diligence to deliver your purpose in life. If you must bring forth your purpose, you must travail in labour which has to do with your diligent pursuit.

Personal responsibility is required to fulfill destiny. You have to accept responsibility for your fulfillment. Responsibility means responding to ability. As I have noted in chapter 8, you have in you the ability in the form of potential given you by God to fulfill your purpose, but you must respond to that ability. Irresponsibility is when you expect everything to be done for you.

Everyone who has achieved any outstanding feat is known to have done something to make it happen. There is no success story without a price diligently paid by the people involved.

Someone once said; "Knowing it is not enough; putting it to work is what makes it work. What you don't pursue, you cannot possess. What you don't run after, you cannot recover."

The classic book on vision, Habakkuk chapter 2, verse 2 says;

And the LORD answered me, and said, Write the vision, and make it plain upon tables, that he may run that readeth it.

This instruction simply means that, it is not enough to write the vision (discovered purpose); to deliver it, the recipient has the responsibility of running with it. He must not sit down with it, he must run with it. In other words, he must pursue the purpose with all diligence in order to deliver it.

A Genius is made by labour, not just by idea. This is because the idea you do not labour to bring to fruition will die unborn.

That is why I believe in what Thomas Edison said that; "Genius is 1% inspiration and 99% perspiration."

Perspiration here connotes sweating in the labour room to bring forth your ideas from God.

However, there are certain factors that are very crucial to the accomplishment of purpose. I have called them the virtues of pursuit. I will take the time to explain three of them one after the other in this segment.

DETERMINATION

Until you are resolutely determined, you cannot accomplish your purpose in life. Your determination is the backbone of your courage which is a requirement for the fulfillment of your purpose. If you are not determined, you cannot deliver you mandate. The reason is that, on your way to fulfillment, you will meet with a lot of challenges that will make your discovery appear as if it is not real.

There is no challenge-free track in life. Therefore, with determination, you will be prepared to confront any challenge that will come your way. With a determined spirit, you will develop a possibility mentality.

The truth of the matter is that if what God told you to do frightens you, it is evident that it is possible to be done and it is accomplishable. As a matter of fact, there is no impossibility with God and for those who believe in His Word and His purpose for their lives.

Mark 9:23;

If thou canst believe, all things are possible to him that believeth.

You need to have this possibility mentality as you maintain your determination to succeed. You need to understand that whatever God commands is as good as done. Your purpose is commanded by God and revealed to you; therefore you should cry to God like Mary "be it unto me according to thy word" (Luke 1:38)

This is because if you believe in what God has told you, you have committed Him for His help in the performance of His Word in your life. (Luke 1:45)

When God told Moses to take over the land of Canaan, he sent out twelve people to spy the land. They went and saw that the land was very good; it was flowing with milk and honey.

However, ten out of the twelve men were men with impossibility mentality because they have no determination to take over the land. The other two men, Joshua and Caleb were men with unusual faith in God. They possess strange order of determination and possibility mentality. They stood their grounds with utmost faith that even though there are giants in that land, as long as God had given it to them, they only needed to go up at once to take it.

At the end of the day, only those two (Joshua and Caleb) made it to Canaan land. The other ten men with all those who believe in their evil report died in the wilderness. (See Numbers chapter 13 and 14)

Specifically, Caleb said in Numbers 13:30;

Let us go up at once, and possess it; for we are well able to overcome it.

God testified concerning Caleb in Numbers 14:24;

But my servant Caleb, because he had another spirit with him, and hath followed me fully, him will I bring into the land whereinto he went; and his seed shall possess it.

When Moses died, Joshua who possessed a determined spirit was given the mantle of leadership over the children of Israel.

God has given you the land of your fulfillment which is your purpose, but you must be determined to go up at once to possess it. You must not fear any challenges on the way because God is with you. You must possess that determined spirit in order to fulfill your purpose.

Abraham Lincoln once said; "Always bear in mind that your own resolution to succeed is more important than any other one thing."

You have to develop that spirit of resolute determination on your way to fulfilling your purpose

PLANNING

Planning is a major factor in the pursuit of any given task. It will be fool-hardy to think that there is no need for man to make plans in order to fulfill divine purpose dwelling on the premise that God has made all the plans for man. Failure to plan is failure to succeed. There is no man who can successfully deliver divine mandate without personal commitment to planning. God plans for no man; planning is man's responsibility. The purpose you do not plan, the object you cannot deliver. God's part is to reveal His purpose to man; it is man's part to plan how to make it a reality.

Proverbs 16:1, 9;

To man belong the plans of the heart, but from the LORD comes the reply of the tongue.

In his heart a man plans his course, but the LORD determines his steps. (NIV)

The man who has discovered his purpose is the one to make the plans for the fulfillment. It is the plan you present to God according to His purpose for you that will determine the kind of help He will send to you. God will help you in your pursuit, but He will only send you help according to the plans you make.

Luke 14:28-30;

For which of you, intending to build a tower, does not sit down first and count the cost, whether he has enough to finish it, lest, after he has laid the foundation, and is not able to finish, all who see it begin to mock him, saying, 'This man began to build and was not able to finish.' (NKJV)

Your discovered purpose is likened to an intention to build a tower. Sitting down first and counting the cost is the planning aspect. You are the one to count the cost, that is, make the plan. In that scripture above, Jesus was showing us the principle required to fulfill destiny.

Brian Tracy said; ***"Every minute you spend in planning saves 10 minutes in execution; this gives you a 1,000 percent Return on Energy!"***

King Solomon who is reputed to be the wisest king in his days brought this picture out very clearly in Proverbs 24:3-4,

When he said; Any enterprise is built by wise planning, becomes strong through common sense, and profits wonderfully by keeping abreast of the facts. (TLB)

In other words, your purpose in likened to an enterprise which requires wise planning, common sense and keeping abreast of the facts. In planning, wisdom is required and it is a product of divine inspiration. Common sense is required which is a product of earthly wisdom, facts are required which are direct products of intellectual wisdom. Planning requires the use of inspired ideas from the Holy Spirit, the knowledge of your environment and acquired knowledge from the academic institution.

It is very important in your planning to have a book where you document you plans; step by step in the order of what you must do to fulfill your purpose. These documented plans must be based on what your purpose in life is by your discovery. Therefore, quality time must be spent in planning all the possibilities of what you must do. You must plan your time, because there is time for everything in life. You must plan your finances, because it is not all money that comes your way that should be spent. You must plan your day as you need to know what to do per time; that is how you can maximize each day of your life. Set goals based on your expectations.

Ken Gaub once said; *"**Your future begins now- with your goal. Success does not require a super intellect. It does require a dream with plans to reach a specific goal.**"*

Your goal is a dream in action, with a purpose. Goals should be out of reach but within sight and it should have deadline. You can never accomplish more than you plan. Planning for the actualization of your purpose is your personal responsibility.

DEDICATION

Dedication is a key factor for the successful pursuit of any given assignment. This is what I have called commitment factor. The purpose you are not committed to, the object you cannot deliver. It is your commitment level today that determines where you will sit tomorrow.

It was Dr. Stephen Covey that said; ***"Without involvement, there is no commitment. Mark it down, asterisk it, circle it, underline it. No involvement, no commitment."***

It is your full involvement in the pursuit of your purpose that ignites your commitment. Jesus, our perfect example in the school of purpose demonstrated a very high level of commitment to His assignment on earth. He took His assignment more important than His physical food. As a matter of fact, He called His assignment His main food.

John 4:34;

Jesus said to them, My food (nourishment) is to do the will (pleasure) of Him Who sent Me and to accomplish and completely finish His work. (AMP)

He did not only talk about doing His work, but to finish it. He gave His entire life to the accomplishment of His mission on earth. Until your assignment becomes more important to you than your physical food, you are not dedicated.

Dedication means deadly commitment. In other words, you have sacrificed your life to become dead to your assignment.

In another instance, Jesus considered His assignment as a work that must be worked out. He did not see Himself resting until He had accomplished His purpose.

John 9:4;

I must work the works of him that sent me, while it is day: the night cometh, when no man can work.

John 5:17;

But Jesus answered them, My Father worketh hitherto, and I WORK.

Jesus emphasized the place of committed work in our bid to fulfill purpose. Work is a MUST if fulfillment is our desire. And how dedicated you are to the work involved in your discovered purpose will determine how quickly you will deliver the objects.

If you see your work as a must, you will dedicate you life to it. I believe that it is very important to dedicate at least 65% of the 24 hours of everyday to the assignment of our God given purpose, because the level of percentage given to dedication determines the rate of delivery.

Paul is another man of unusual dedication. He was literally dead to his assignment. Through out his life since the time he encountered God's purpose, he sowed himself as a seed that died in the ground of commitment (Philippians 1:21). He worked himself to the finishing line. He even placed himself under an oath of committer just to see to the end of his assignment (2 Timothy 4:7-8).

Paul poured himself out like a drink offering until he finished his assignment. He died empty without taking his potential to the cemetery. I believe that this is the best way to end life.

You need to ask yourself the question; **"What is the percentage of my commitment to the purpose of God for my life"?**

Only you can answer that question, but just be sincere and if you know that you did not measure up to the standard of Jesus in your commitment level, adjust now. You should create time for everything that must be done in order to fulfill your purpose in life. Only those who are dedicated to their God given purpose can accomplish it with speed.

With the rate at which you are pursuing your purpose, will you be able to say that you have finished what God sent you here to do? Are you pouring yourself out like a drink offering? Are you sure that you will not add to the wealth in the cemetery at the end of your life?

It is never late to begin. A dedicated life is a life that will accomplish divine purpose. It is only when you fall into the ground and die that you can bring forth much fruits. (John 12:24)

Chapter 8: DISCIPLINE OF PURPOSE

You will never be the person you can be if pressure and discipline are taken out of your life. - James G. Bulley

Disciplining yourself to do what you know is right and important, although difficult, is the highroad to pride, self-esteem, and personal satisfaction. - Brian Tracy

By constant self-discipline and self-control you can develop greatness of character. - Grenville Kleiser

Fulfillment of destiny is at the mercy of a disciplined lifestyle. When you live a lawless life, you end up having an unfulfilled life. This is because; God will not do what He has commanded you to do in order to fulfill your purpose. He will definitely do His own part and He will supply you with the grace required to do your own part, but He will not do your part. A successful life is anchored on covenant walk. And covenant is a deed between two parties signed, sealed and delivered with an oath. God operates with man on this basis. He is the covenantor, that is, the maker of covenant while man is the covenantee, that is, the beneficiary of the covenant.

It means that God has drafted an agreement between Himself and man. In that agreement, there is what He will do and there is what man must do. God's part is always sure, but most times, man's part is not sure. The reason is that God is constant while man is variable. Fulfillment of divine purpose is a covenant walk between God and man. God's part is that He established a purpose and created man to fulfill it.

However, man's part is to understand this truth, seek to discover his purpose, prepare himself through various means, take the steps required to pursue that purpose with all diligence. But all these aspect will require discipline if it must be successfully done.

WHAT IS DISCIPLINE?

Discipline can be defined as the ability to behave in a controlled and calm manner even in a difficult or stressful situation. It is mental self-control used in directing or changing behavior, learning something, or training for something.

Discipline is the act of placing oneself under certain laws, rules, standard and restrictions. It is making a choice of what needs to be done and what should not be done as a result of ones expectations. In this context discipline means, self imposed standards and restriction. It is the ability to choose between what is lawful and what is expedient.

1 Corinthians 6:12;

All things are lawful unto me, but all things are not expedient: all things are lawful for

me, but I will not be brought under the power of any.

A disciplined man is one who can make the right choice between the two. It is not all things that are lawful that are beneficial. The ability to choose between the two is what determines ones level of discipline. As someone on a mission, you must make it a point of duty to live under certain laws and restrictions. You need to have a standard by which you live, because, fulfillment of purpose is determined by how disciplined you are.

When you have discovered your purpose in life, you are initiated into leadership, but fulfillment of that purpose will be determined by the standard and restrictions under which you place yourself.

There is time for everything in life and when you are not doing what you need to do at the time you are suppose to do it, you are not disciplined.

There is no future for an undisciplined person and the depth of your discipline determines your command of leadership. To achieve your desired aim or goal in life, you must become a law to yourself. God gave you the assignment and He expects you to fulfill it, but what you do with it is what determines whether you will fulfill it or not.

From my studies over the years, I have come to realize that, it is not enough to know where you belong in God's master plan; but it is much more important to be disciplined enough to stay there.

Many things will contend for your attention in life, but with a disciplined lifestyle, you will know what you must give your attention to in order to fulfill your purpose.

The ability to discipline yourself to delay gratification in the short term in order to enjoy greater rewards in the long term, is the indispensable prerequisite for success.

Discipline in Prayer Life

Prayer is the channel by which we constantly grant God permission to intervene on our behalf in the pursuit of divine purpose. Prayer is our communication channel by which we secure God's help without which we cannot accomplish His purpose in life.

It is very important that we maintain a disciplined prayer life if fulfillment of destiny is our desire. As a matter of fact, prayerlessness is a display of pride, because; when you are not prayerful, you are invariably telling God that you did not need His help in your affairs.

Jesus, our perfect example showed us with practical illustration how important it is for us to take prayer with utmost seriousness if we must accomplish success in whatever we are involved in (Luke 18:1).

Also, He recommended at least one hour prayer for us on a daily basis, as revealed in His statement to Peter in Mark 14:37; And he cometh, and findeth them sleeping, and saith unto Peter, Simon, sleepest thou? couldest not thou watch one hour ?

In another instance, Paul, who is a man known to have fulfilled God's purpose for his life showed us that prayer is a major key to fulfilling divine purpose. The secrets of men are in their stories. Paul was a disciplined man in the aspect of prayer.

Ephesians 6:18;

Praying always with all prayer and supplication in the Spirit, and watching thereunto with all perseverance and supplication for all saints;

Friend, you must be disciplined in your prayer life if you desire to fulfill God's purpose for your life. Spend at least one hour everyday in thanksgiving, praise and prayer in order to maintain a sound spiritual life. And as you grow in grace, you will spend more hours in God's presence, because you will always long for fellowship with Him everyday.

Discipline in Word Study

The wisdom of God is a major key to fulfilling His purpose in life. No matter how great the vision or dream you have as your discovered purpose, without the wisdom of God, you cannot accomplish it. And the Word of God is a major channel for us to encounter the wisdom of God.

It is a well known fact that, the wisdom of a man is discovered from the words of that man. In the same way, the wisdom of God is found in His word. The wisdom of God is the ability to know what to do from God and doing it.

You need to maintain a disciplined life of committed Word study on a daily basis in order to locate the wisdom for your fulfillment. You must place yourself under a law to study God's Word everyday, particularly early in the morning. If you make it a law to yourself, it becomes your daily lifestyle and you will always know what to do per time as you pursue your purpose. (1 Timothy 4:13)

Proper attention must be given to constant reading and studying of the Word of God everyday as we pursue our God given purpose. This is how we can continue to receive from God the instructions needed to successfully carry out the assignment He gave us. (2 Timothy 2:15).

Your spiritual life needs to grow daily as you pursue God's purpose and one major way for that to happen is by committed Word study. Be disciplined to study the Word daily.

Discipline in Reading of Relevant Books

One major area where we need to be discipline is in our commitment to the reading of relevant books. You will eventually become like the author whose books you read because; you learn and acquire the kind of wisdom possessed by that author.

Where you will find yourself tomorrow is determined by the books you are reading today. If you are going to fulfill your purpose, you need to build a library of books which are relevant to what you are pursuing.

Many years ago I heard the story of a young man who read a little book and saw what the author wrote about starting small and growing big. He took that knowledge and began as a boy to do something small. He grew up from there and today, Richard

Branson, is the founder of Virgin Empire, a conglomerate. He is rated as one of the wealthiest in the world. He got the knowledge from reading a book.

Every man who is a reference today has references. If you must become a man of impact as you fulfill your purpose, you must be committed to the reading books that are relevant to your assignment.

Be disciplined to learn from men that know more than you in your area of pursuit. You can only see farther than others when you stand on the shoulder of those who have gone ahead of you.

Paul became the greatest of all the apostles by his discipline and commitment to the reading of books. He became more knowledgeable than all the others.

2 Timothy 4:13;

The cloke that I left at Troas with Carpus, when thou comest, bring with thee, and the books, but especially the parchments.

Paul possessed a high level of mental dignity by his commitment to books, and he finished his course on earth. You need to discipline yourself to the reading of relevant books everyday to gain new knowledge as you pursue your purpose.

Discipline in Spoken Words

A man is a reflection of his spoken words and the words you speak today are what determine what becomes of your tomorrow. You are either going forward or going backward based on what you keep saying. God's purpose for your life is sure as far as God is concerned, but the reality of it is determined by you and one of the ways you determine it in by what you keep saying.

Proverbs 6:2;

Thou art snared with the words of thy mouth, thou art taken with the words of thy mouth.

Many people have been destroyed because of what they have said in times past. But the same mouth can reverse any negative situation. If you do not know how to talk, you cannot know how to live. How you live is determined by how you speak. Your words will either make you or mar you; therefore, your destiny is in your hands based on the words you keep speaking.

What comes to you is what you keep speaking to yourself. A man cannot grow beyond the level of his spoken words. Therefore, if you want to go up in life, discipline yourself to keep speaking positive and life-transforming words that relate to your desire (Proverbs 12:14).

The good that comes your way is the good you speak to yourself. In the same way, the evil that comes is the evil you speak. As a matter of fact, the words of your mouth are what bring forth the fruits of your labour (Proverbs 13:2-3).

It is wisdom to know when to talk and when not to talk. That is why it takes discipline to fulfill destiny. Discipline in the area of what you say with your mouth is very important as you keep pursuing your purpose.

Joshua 6:10;

And Joshua had commanded the people, saying, Ye shall not shout, nor make any

noise with your voice, neither shall any word proceed out of your mouth, until the day I bid you shout; then shall ye shout.

God gave Joshua that commandment to the Israelites; a time to speak and a time not to speak. A time to shout and a time not to shout. That is how God operates with His people. But it takes discipline to be able to know the timing.

In another instance, God told His people to open their mouth wide as we have it recorded in

Psalm 81:10;

I am the LORD thy God, which brought thee out of the land of Egypt: open thy mouth wide, and I will fill it.

If you keep quiet when God tells you to talk, you will miss the blessing He has for you at that time and if you talk when He told you to keep quiet, you will miss His blessing.

Also, it is very important not to allow corrupt or evil communication because such can truncate ones destiny. Paul admonished very strongly in

Ephesians 4:29;

Let no corrupt communication proceed out of your mouth, but that which is good to the use of edifying, that it may minister grace unto the hearers.

I believe that one of the reasons is that the angels attend to the words of our mouth, just as they attend to the word of God.

Ecclesiastes 5:6;

Suffer not thy mouth to cause thy flesh to sin; neither say thou before the angel, that it was an error: wherefore should God be angry at thy voice, and destroy the work of thine hands?

Friend, the words of your mouth will either ignite God's blessing or His anger, depending on what you say, how you say it, the time you say it and where you say it. Be disciplined with your words, it determines a lot of things in your life.

Discipline in Sleeping

Sleep is very good for our health, but excess of it is dangerous to the fulfillment of divine purpose. A man on a mission must know when to sleep and when to be awake. It is not every night season that is meant for sleeping. Although, night season is designed for sleep, it takes discipline to be able to tame the body to be awake in the night from time to time, because certain spiritual battles are fought and won by night.

Your purpose is supposed to bring you into prosperity, but indiscipline from sleeping ends a man in poverty as Solomon noted in Proverbs 6:9-11;

How long wilt thou sleep, O sluggard? when wilt thou arise out of thy sleep?

Yet a little sleep, a little slumber, a little folding of the hands to sleep:

So shall thy poverty come as one that travelleth, and thy want as an armed man.

Most of the time, we are able to pick the voice of God needed for our fulfillment in the silence of the night or very early morning. When you are still fast asleep at such times, how will you be able to pick that instruction from God?

In all my years of study of greatness, I have found out that, most great men are made by commitment to seeking God in the night season.

Nehemiah, who was instrumental to the rebuilding of the broken down wall of Jerusalem, used the night season to secure the wisdom needed to accomplish the work.

Nehemiah 2:11-13, 15;

So I came to Jerusalem, and was there three days.

And I arose in the night, I and some few men with me; neither told I any man what my God had put in my heart to do at Jerusalem: neither was there any beast with me, save the beast that I rode upon.

And I went out by night by the gate of the valley, even before the dragon well, and to the dung port, and viewed the walls of Jerusalem, which were broken down, and the gates thereof were consumed with fire.

Then went I up in the night by the brook, and viewed the wall, and turned back, and entered by the gate of the valley, and so returned.

By utilizing the night season to view the broken down wall, he was able to know how to get the work done.

Also, the secret that turned Daniel and his three friends to celebrities was revealed to him in a night vision. They took the time to seek God in prayer in the night season.

Daniel 2:19;

Then was the secret revealed unto Daniel in a night vision. Then Daniel blessed the God of heaven.

Daniel and his friends were on the verge of being killed by the wicked king, but God intervened by providing a solution to the king's problem through Daniel. What if Daniel and his friends were sleeping at that time? They would have died with others.

Jesus, in His statement in Matthew 13:25, revealed that the enemy of man's destiny always shows up while man is sleeping. And most times, sleeping is in the night.

But while men slept , his enemy came and sowed tares among the wheat, and went his way.

You must be awake at night to deal with the enemy of your fulfillment of destiny.

The secret of fulfillment of Paul was revealed in his commitment to visions of the night. On several occasions, God revealed secrets to him about very important issues in his pursuit.

Acts 16:9;

And a vision appeared to Paul in the night; There stood a man of Macedonia, and prayed him, saying, Come over into Macedonia, and help us.

Visions and revelations required to fulfill destiny come most times by night. And it takes discipline to be awake in the night so as to fulfill divine purpose.

Discipline in Time Management

What you spend time on determines what comes out of your life. Since purpose is the most important thing in life, it is very important that we allot the highest percentage of our time to doing the things that will contribute to the fulfillment of our purpose.

It was Dr. Mike Murdock that said; ***"What you do daily determines what you become permanently."***

How much time do you spend in pursuing your purpose? How do you manage your daily hours? Discipline is required in this area of your life because; the more time you invest into doing those things that will aid the fulfillment of your purpose, the faster you will accomplish it. And the faster, the better, so that you can move on to the next phase of your assignment until you fully deliver you divine mandate on earth.

There is time for everything in life. I believe that we need to learn how to plan each hour of the day (Ecclesiastes 3:1).

We can do that successfully by allotting different tasks to different hours of the day and measure the completion of each task on the agenda. Create a daily agenda on a daily basis, but learn how to prioritize. What that means is that we should put the first thing first before the next thing in the order of importance.

The Management expert, Peter Drucker once said; ***"Time is the scarcest resource and unless it is managed nothing else can be managed."***

Discipline is required in how you manage your time.

Discipline in Handling Finance

Money is a part of life. There will not be successful existence without the use of money. To buy any thing, money is needed. To fulfill divine purpose, money is needed. You will have to buy most of the things you need to carry out God's mandate for your life. That is why, there has to be a source of financial income as you pursue your purpose. I am not saying that we are living because of money; No! We are living for purpose. But money is one of the tools required to fulfill that purpose.

Discipline is needed to know what money to spend on what, how must it to be spent and why it has to be spent on it.

Also, it is important to learn how to save from your income. There are things to purchase and you will be able to buy that thing from your savings. No matter how little, learn to save.

In addition, by all means, avoid waste. Wastage of resource cuts short the fulfillment of destiny. Even the vital part of ones live can be lost to waste resulting from indiscipline in handling financial resources.

The Prodigal son would have lost his life and destiny, had he not returned to his father after he had wasted all his money.

Luke 15:13-14;

And not many days after the younger son gathered all together, and took his journey into a far country, and there wasted his substance with riotous living.

And when he had spent all, there arose a mighty famine in that land; and he began to be in want.

Lack and want result from wastage as we can see in the life of the prodigal son.

Prudence in financial management is part of the requirements for fulfilling divine purpose. Therefore, discretion is needed in how we handle money.

In his book, Rich Dad, Poor Dad, Robert Kiyosaki said; **"Money without financial intelligence is money soon gone."**

There is need to acquire financial intelligence as you go on in the pursuit of your purpose.

Friend, I believe that we all need to subscribe to the various areas of discipline as explained in this chapter. Discipline in all areas of human endeavours has a lot to do in determining whether purpose is fulfilled or not.

Chapter 9: ASSOCIATION DIMENSIONS

Choose your friends with caution; plan your future with purpose, and frame your life with faith. - Thomas S. Monson

The relationships you are engaged in will either pull you forward or pull you backward. There is no middle. People either help you grow or hold you back. - Dan Reiland

We are far more liable to catch the vices than the virtues of our associates. - Denis Diderot

Two young boys, Dave and Charley were childhood friends. They were together in the church choir, doing very well as well behaved boys. As they were moving on attending bible class and preparing for the work of the ministry, Dave suddenly changed his mind. He met another guy somehow and went into worldly music and became a secular hip hop singer. He was still using the gift of God in him but now in a negative way because; he was no longer in the centre of God's purpose for his life.

After many years, Charley, who continued in the school of ministry, grew to become a well respected pastor over the same church where he was singing in the choir with Dave, his childhood friend. Dave who changed his company and left the church has lost his salvation and now fully involved with drunkard, smokers and drug pushers. Although the church members did their best to get him restored all through the years but all efforts proved abortive.

Today Charley is fulfilling God's purpose as a pastor whose ministry is bringing many souls into the kingdom of God. On the other hand, Dave is out of touch with God's purpose for his life, because he was keeping a wrong company.

There is power in association in determining the fulfillment of divine purpose. It is very important to understand that, in the pursuit of purpose, people are needed. And as a matter of fact, your purpose makes you someone needed by people. Therefore, to succeed in fulfilling your purpose, you need people and people need you. You cannot succeed alone and you cannot live in isolation. You must relate with people.

You cannot go on the journey of fulfilling of your destiny alone. Even God was not alone at creation in the beginning. It took the combined efforts of the trinity, that is, God the Father, the Son and the Holy Spirit to bring forth everything on earth.

Specifically, when it was time to create man, God did not say; Let me..., rather, He said; Let us make man... (Genesis 1:26). That statement connotes a combined efforts being put to work.

Also, the first thing that God found fault with after creation was man. Earlier on after creation, it was said in

Genesis 1:31;

And God saw every thing that he had made, and, behold, it was very good.

However, a time came when God wanted man to fulfill his purpose in the garden where he was put as the king on earth; God had to review his program. Then, He discovered that there is no way man can fully deliver his assignment being alone.

And the LORD God said, It is not good that the man should be alone... (Genesis 2:18)

God, who said that the creation of man is very good, is the same God who said it is not good for that man to be alone. He did not only discover the problem, He provided the solution immediately, by creating a suitable partner for the man. (Genesis 2:21-23)

There is a suitable helper you need for the fulfillment of your destiny because; God has designed life to be a contact spot where networking of people determines success and/or failure in man's destiny.

But, the relationships you keep determine the realities of your life. And the company you keep determines the outcome of your life. Where you will end tomorrow is determined by the kind of people you associate with today.

Many great destinies have been fulfilled as a result of relationships, while many did not get fulfilled because of relationships. There are dreams and visions that never became a reality because of wrong relationship.

King Solomon revealed this truth in a statement he made in

Proverbs 13:20;

He that walketh with wise men shall be wise: but a companion of fools shall be destroyed.

However, King Solomon became the wisest man in his days because he was keeping company with the only wise God and other godly people. (1 Kings 3:3-13; 4:29-34). He loved God as he was keeping company with Him constantly.

But a time came in his life that he changed his company to wrong and foolish ones and he ended up becoming a foolish man. His swapped loving God with loving strange women and that attracted the anger of God upon him. That wrong association corrupted his wisdom. (1 Kings 11:1-14)

Paul corroborates this truth in his epistle to the Corinthian church when he wrote in

`1st Corinthians 15:33; Be not deceived: evil communications corrupt good manners.

The Amplified version puts it more clearly;

Do not be so deceived and misled! Evil companionships (communion, associations) corrupt and deprave good manners and morals and character. (1 Corinthians 15:33 AMP)

The word communication in that verse means company, association, close relationship and communion. When the company or association is evil, it will corrupt your good manners and moral characters which are the keys to a glorious destiny. On the other hand, if you keep a good company or association, it will improve your good matters and moral characters in enhancing the fulfillment of your destiny.

I believe that the people you closely relate with have a lot to contribute to your life, either positively or negatively. You will always imbibe the wisdom or foolishness of your close associates. That is why care must be taken to choose the company we keep. Because anyone you relate with who is not increasing you will inevitably decrease you.

I like the way George Washington put it when he said **"Be courteous to all, but intimate with**

few; and let those be well-tried before you give them your confidence."

Friendship is not by force; rather, it is a choice you make, because friends differ. You should be able to pinpoint those friends that truly stimulate, educate and placate you. You must carefully select those who you know will contribute positively in helping to fulfill your God given purpose.

It is a display of foolishness to associate closely with anyone who has nothing to add to you. People like that will take you far away from the pursuit of your purpose, because, if they are not adding to you, they are subtracting from you. If I know the people you have as friends and close associates today, I can predict where you will be in future. This is because;

you will always 'catch' the spirit of those you closely relate with.

Charles 'Tremendous' Jones once said; ***"You'll remain the same way you are today in five years, except for two things: the books you read and the people with whom you walk."***

As you go on in the pursuit of your purpose, you must be careful who you share your vision, dream and challenges with. There are vision destroyers and dream killers. As a matter of fact, there are people you will share your vision with and they will tell you to never dare it because, to them it is not accomplishable.

I remember the story of these two Microsoft partners; Bill Gates and Paul Allen. These two guys have been friends since when they were children. They relate very closely as people of like minds and today, they are both multibillionaires as listed by Forbes Inc.

If you are going about with someone who is not purpose-driven, even if you have discovered your own purpose, you might end up not fulfilling it. Because there are tendencies that he will mislead you to be like him. People who are doing nothing always look for those who will join them in doing nothing.

However, associations have different levels and each level is very important to the fulfillment of our God given purpose in life.

Friendship and Companionship

This level of association is one of the most important aspects of relationship in the pursuit of divine purpose. When God reveals to you or when you discover your purpose in life, there are people that God will position in your way as friends or companions. Although, that relationship has to grow depending on the benefits accruing to each party involved.

A friend is someone who is emotionally close to you; someone who thinks well of you or in good terms with you. He must be somebody who can learn from you and you can learn from. He is someone you can share your life issues with and will be available for you at all times.

David and Jonathan's relationship is a very good example of what friendship is all about. They became so close to each other and bared each other's burdens.

1 Samuel 18:1, 3, 4;

And it came to pass, when he had made an end of speaking unto Saul, that the soul of Jonathan was knit with the soul of David, and Jonathan loved him as his own soul.

Then Jonathan and David made a covenant, because he loved him as his own soul.

And Jonathan stripped himself of the robe that was upon him, and gave it to David, and his garments, even to his sword, and to his bow, and to his girdle.

They made covenant of eternal friendship because their souls were knit together.

God used the friendship of Jonathan and David to establish the kingship of David over Israel. In other words, David was able to fulfill that aspect of his God given purpose because of his friendship with Jonathan.

Also, Daniel and his three friends; Shadrach, Meshach and Abednego were able to fulfill destiny because of their close companionship. When Daniel was faced with difficult situation, he shared it with his friends (Daniel 2:16-19).

These four young men combined effort to secure wisdom solution to the problem of the pagan king and they got it. In most cases, combined efforts are required to solve the problems of life.

Ecclesiastes 4:9-10;

Two are better than one; because they have a good reward for their labour.

For if they fall, the one will lift up his fellow: but woe to him that is alone when he falleth; for he hath not another to help him up.

Two good heads are better than one. From the lives of David and Jonathan; Daniel and his three friends, we can see the power of positive friendship.

God might have given you a business dream or vision as your own discovered purpose. It is possible that you do not have the cash to pursue that dream; but the finance for that dream is in the hands of someone and it could be your friends. You do not really need to go and obtain a loan from the bank; rather, you can partner with that friend of yours and agree on profit sharing ratio. But you need to be sure that you are relating with someone who is of like mind.

To keep building my success, I make sure I associate with other successful people. No man is an island. The journey to success is a team effort. Success breeds success. This is why the rich get richer. If you want to become rich, then you need to hang out with the rich.

However, if you want to change yourself or your lifestyle, then it may be time to change the people you associate with, because, a big part of who you are is determined by the people you hang out with.

Jim Rohn once said; "You must constantly ask yourself these questions: Who am I around? What are they doing to me? What have they got me reading? What have they got me saying? Where do they have me going? What do they have me thinking? And most important, what do they have me becoming? Then ask yourself the big question: Is that okay? Your life does not get better by chance, it gets better by change."

The people around you determine what you are becoming. If you hang around negative people, you become a negative person. If they are positive, you become a better and positive person.

Proverbs 27:17;

Iron sharpeneth iron; so a man sharpeneth the countenance of his friend.

Your friends have a lot to do in your life; that is why you must make a wise choice for good and purpose-driven friendship. When you use iron to strike another iron, you will discover that the sparks that fly from that contact are very stimulating, especially when it is done in a dark place. That is how stimulating and refreshing it is when there is mutual and purpose-driven networking between two friends.

Mentorship

Fulfillment of destiny requires having a mentor. Mentoring involves accepting a perfect knowledge from an imperfect man. Your mentor is someone who constantly relates with you to teach you what you need to know in order to fully deliver your mandate on earth.

A mentor is somebody, usually older and more experienced, who advises and guides a younger, less experienced person. There is need for a mentor-protégé relationship in our bid to carry out the assignment that God has given us. This is because, even though each one has a peculiar purpose, we have similar assignment required to fulfill our God given purpose. Also, there are virtues required to fulfill God's purpose which are common to all men who desire to accomplish purpose. These virtues are learnable and transferable from those who have them to those who desire to have them.

There are people with proven results in the area of your own calling or discovered purpose, who have accomplished great exploits. All you need to do is receive one or more of them as your mentor(s), so that you can learn from them how you can fulfill your own purpose.

Mentor-protégé relationship is like climbing on the shoulders of giants so that you can see farther. There are many things you cannot know except you learn it from someone. Or is there anything in life that we can claim to know without learning it?

I believe that every man is a bundle of knowledge gained from other men. That is how God designed life to be. He places men in different positions to be sources of inspiration to others. Every great man is made by another great man.

My mentor in ministry, Dr David Oyedepo once said; *"Every success story is a product of another success story. Giants are born of giants."*

The great Prophet Moses surrendered to the mentoring counsel of his father in law, Jethro. Moses was operating his ministry in a way that was very tasking on his life. I believe that he thought since he was the one that God called, he had to be only one to attend to all the people. How can one man attend to the need of about three million people all alone? He was actually doing this until the time that Jethro, his father in law visited him and witnessed how Moses was operating (Exodus 18:17-19, 24).

Moses would have died earlier than the time he died, because he was wearing himself out as he was the only one attending to all the people. But when he took the counsel of his God sent mentor, Jethro his father in law, he lived long and fulfilled God's purpose for his life.

Also, Joshua was able to fulfill God's purpose for his life by reason of his long standing mentor-protégé relationship with Moses. And before the death of Moses, Joshua received the impartation of the spirit of wisdom upon Moses by which he was able to continue from where Moses stopped.

Deuteronomy 34:9;

And Joshua the son of Nun was full of the spirit of wisdom; for Moses had laid his hands upon him: and the children of Israel hearkened unto him, and did as the LORD commanded Moses.

Joshua 1:1-2;

Now after the death of Moses the servant of the LORD it came to pass, that the LORD

spake unto Joshua the son of Nun, Moses' minister, saying,

Moses my servant is dead; now therefore arise, go over this Jordan, thou, and all this people, unto the land which I do give to them, even to the children of Israel.

In another instance, Elijah's mentor-protégé relationship with Elisha was responsible for the fulfillment of Elisha's God given purpose. He followed Elijah to the end of his life and at the end; he succeeded in partaking of the double portion of the spirit upon Elijah. (2 Kings 2:1-15)

In the case of Jesus and the twelve apostles, they were with Him as His protégés. He was teaching them ministry for three and half years. By the time He left for heaven, they continued from where He stopped in circulating the gospel to the nations of the world. (Read the gospel of Matthew, Mark, Luke, John and Acts of the Apostles for details)

Also, Paul, the great apostle with unusual depth of revelation of God, had a young man Timothy as his associate who served with him as his protégé in ministry. Timothy ended up as the first Bishop of the church in Ephesus. He fulfilled God's purpose for his life by reason of the mentor-protégé relationship he had with Paul. (1Timothy 1:2, 18, 2 Timothy 1:2).

On several occasions, Timothy received impartation of grace from Paul by laying on of his hand. Therefore, he was able to operate with the same kind of grace upon Paul. (1 Timothy 4:14, 2 Timothy 1:6)

However, in some cases, you have to serve under the leadership of your mentor just like in the case of Moses-Joshua, Elijah-Elisha, Jesus-The 12 Apostles and Paul-Timothy.

Also, you can choose a mentor by proxy. In that case, all you need to do is locate the books and DVD, VCD, CD, and MP3 of the person you have chosen as your mentor and learn all you need to learn from him by reading his books and listening to his tapes.

It was William Ellery Channing that once said; **"Every man is a volume if you know how to read him."**

The results in terms of exploits and great achievements in the lives of men are mostly the determining factors in choosing a mentor. Another factor is a discovery of what you need to achieve in your life.

Also, the character of your mentor matters a lot. A good mentor is someone who is interested in your success, not someone who talks much about his our achievement.

Lord Bacon once said; **"The less people speak of their greatness, the more we think of it."**

Those who are great indeed talk less of their greatness because of their interest in the greatness of others. If your discovered purpose has to do with providing business solutions, then you need a mentor who is providing business solutions. If your own is leadership, then you need a mentor who is involved in leadership development.

If you are a pastor, hang around pastors with testimonies in their ministries. If you are a teacher by divine purpose, hang around teachers who know more than you so that you can learn how to be a better teacher.

For instance, as a Pastor and leadership coach by virtue of my discovered purpose, I have a Pastor and leadership trainer as my spiritual father and mentor. Also, I relate very closely with some other pastors and leadership coaches who have achieved great things in life and ministry in different parts of the world as I read their books and watch their DVDs from time to time.

Friend, understand that the fulfillment of your destiny is a product of the kind of relationship you keep at every stage of your life. As you move on in life you will come across different kinds of people, some are positive while others are negative. You need to be careful to choose who you will relate and associate with. Take the time to study people before you share your dream, vision and ideas with them. You will be held responsible for fulfillment or otherwise of your destiny.

I will conclude this chapter with the words of the great man, Dr. Stephen Covey who said; **"One of the best ways to educate our hearts is to look at our interaction with other people, because our relationships with others are fundamentally a reflection of our relationship with ourselves."**

Having come with me thus far in this book, I am very sure that you will make a decision right now that will determine where you will be in the next five, ten, twenty, thirty, forty and more years. That decision is about choosing to associate wisely in the area of friendship and mentorship. It will determine your fulfillment in life.

Chapter 10: PATIENCE OF PURPOSE

If I have ever made any valuable discoveries, it has been owing more to patient attention, than to any other talent. - Isaac Newton

Learn the art of patience. Apply discipline to your thoughts when they become anxious over the outcome of a goal. Impatience breeds anxiety, fear, discouragement and failure. Patience creates confidence, decisiveness, and a rational outlook, which eventually leads to success. - Brian Adams

The virtue of patience is a fundamental requirement in the fulfillment of divine purpose. Until patience is in place, you are not a candidate for a fulfilled destiny. Every one who has ever accomplished any great thing in the world has been known to possess this great virtue of patience.

To keep doing the same thing over and over again in an attempt to solve a particular problem, patience is required. Without patience, you cannot be diligent in your pursuit and without diligence, fulfillment is not in view. Patience is of utmost important in the race of life. It takes patience to persist and persevere in the pursuit of divine purpose until the end.

The purpose of God for your life is speaking of what will happen in your life in the nearest future. That great vision, dream or revelation which gave you a sense of divine purpose, will not happen immediately as you may think. Be very careful not to truncate God's purpose for your life as a result of haste and impatience.

WHAT IS PATIENCE?

Patience means

- capacity to endure - ability to endure waiting

- capacity for persevering calmly especially when faced with difficulties

 - forbearance

Patience is the ability to endure and persevere calmly in the face of difficult situations in order to accomplish a set objective, aim or goal. It is a virtue that keeps one going until the purpose is fulfilled.

It is very important to note that God's purpose has its timing and its timing is the right time. In other words, there is a due season for every divine program and that due season is God-determined.

Habakkuk 2:2-3;

And the Lord said to me, "Write my answer on a billboard, large and clear, so that anyone can read it at a glance and rush to tell the others.

But these things I plan won't happen right away. Slowly, steadily, surely, the time approaches when the vision will be fulfilled. If it seems slow, do not despair, for these things will surely come to pass. Just be patient! They will not be overdue a single day! (TLB)

Many have lost out of fulfillment of divine purpose by impatience. There is no substitute for patience in the race of destiny. Verse three of the scripture above paints a very graphic picture of how important patience is in our bid to deliver divine purpose.

...these things I plan won't happen right away. Slowly, steadily, surely, the time approaches when the vision will be fulfilled. If it seems slow, do not despair, for these things will surely come to pass. Just be patient! They will not be overdue a single day.

In other words, that purpose that you have discovered will take time before it will be fulfilled. It will not happen immediately, but slowly, steadily and surely it will be fully fulfilled. It is your responsibility not to despair, but to patiently wait for it as you pursue it. And you will discover that it will not be overdue for a single day when the time comes.

Ecclesiastes 3:1;

There is a right time for everything: (TLB)

There is a time to discover divine purpose. There is a time for preparation for its pursuit. There is a time to begin the full pursuit of the purpose. Also, there is a time to move from one phase to the next phase. That is how God programmed everything in life.

Your purpose is like a living being that grows and develops from one stage to another until it is fully grown. It is like a seed planted which goes through the process of growth phase by phase until it becomes a fully grown tree from which one can eat fruits.

Just like there is no born adult. Every adult was born as a baby and grows to become an adult with time, not over night. In the same way, your purpose is like a new born baby when you discover it. It will require time to grow and deliver its contents phase by phase. The day you discover your purpose is the birthday of your purpose and assignment in life. As you begin to pursue it, you will need patience to wait for it to bring forth its fruits phase by phase.

John Quincy Adams once said; "Patience and perseverance have a magical effect before which difficulties disappear and obstacles vanish."

God specializes in showing us the end from the beginning. (Isaiah 46:9-11). Then He sets up a program that will get us to that revealed end. But we must not expect to get to that end immediately, because there is need to prepare for all the in-between responsibilities to get there. We must be careful not to throw in the towel just because it did not happen according to our own time table. But with patience, we will move from stage to stage until we get there. It is just a matter of time.

Luke 8:15;

But that on the good ground are they, which in an honest and good heart, having heard the word, keep it, and bring forth fruit with patience.

Fruitfulness in fulfillment of divine purpose will answer to patience. Also, your purpose in life is the race that God has set before you to run. Life is a race and every one has a peculiar race set before him by God. It is the discovery of your purpose that puts you in that race. In other words, you have no race to run in life until you have discovered you own God ordained purpose.

Hebrews 12:1;

...and let us run with patience the race that is set before us.

In as much as the race that God has set before each one of us begins with the discovery of our life's purpose, it is imperative for us to understand that patience is required for us to run that race successfully.

Paul admonished that we run with patience the race that is set before us.

That means, running our individual race in life needs patience to determine whether we obtain the prize or not.

The great hero of faith, Kenneth E. Hagin once said; ***"God doesn't tell us His whole plan for us all at once. Often, He can tell us only bits and pieces of His plan because we wouldn't be*** *able to understand or bear more than a glimpse of what He has in store for us. A person has to be patient to wait for God to bring to pass His purpose in his life. There is a time and a season for all things and the time is not always now."*

God sometimes brings things forth in our lives in seed form because He is a God of process and process takes time. We need to submit to divine process which is not easy most times. We must all pass the test of patience in our bid to fulfill God's purpose as we surrender to His process.

The world's population is close to seven billion now, but God began with one man, Adam. Also, God showed Abraham how uncountable his seed would be just like the stars in the sky and the sand on the sea shore, but he started with one, Isaac who was born after he had patiently endured for twenty-five years.

Hebrews 6:12-15;

That ye be not slothful, but followers of them who through faith and patience inherit the promises.

For when God made promise to Abraham, because he could swear by no greater, he sware by himself,

Saying, Surely blessing I will bless thee, and multiplying I will multiply thee.

And so, after he had patiently endured, he obtained the promise.

He did not get to the fulfillment of his purpose over night; neither did he obtain it by faith only, he got it after he had patiently endured.

Joseph was shown his future as a great leader, but he started as a slave in Potiphar's house. And he ended up as a great leader over the nation of Egypt.

David was ordained to be a king over Israel, but he started as shepherd boy in his father's farm.

Jesus was sent by God to save the whole world from sin, but He started with 12 disciples and today billions are saved worldwide calling Jesus their Lord.

Everything ordained by God to be great always begins small, but it takes patience to work through that small beginning to greatness. Without patience, the fortitude to continue with persistence may be lost along the way. God wants that small beginning to increase greatly (Job 8:7)

There is always an appointed time for the full delivery of every purpose and patience is a major key that will get you through to that appointed time.

When Job was attacked, he understood the importance of patience in order to experience a turn around. Therefore, he endured in the time of trouble until the appointed time of God for his change. That was why he affirmed in

Job 14:14;

...all the days of my appointed time will I wait, till my change come.

In as much as Job experienced his desired change through patience, your own time of change will not be delayed for a single day.

James made a reference to Job's experience in James 5:7, 11;

Be patient therefore, brethren, unto the coming of the Lord. Behold, the husbandman waiteth for the precious fruit of the earth, and hath long patience for it, until he receive the early and latter rain.

Behold, we count them happy which endure. Ye have heard of the patience of Job, and have seen the end of the Lord; that the Lord is very pitiful, and of tender mercy.

Just as a farmer needs to wait patiently for his crops to yield harvest, in the same way we need patience to achieve the object of God's purpose for us. No farmer plants a seed today and expects to reap harvest the next day. He needs to wait until the time appointed for the crop to become harvestable. As a matter of fact, long patience is the key to the fulfillment of destiny.

THE FRUITS OF PATIENCE

Every virtue of life has great benefits. Patience is a virtue in fulfilling destiny and among its benefits are:

Focus On End Product

Patience helps one to maintain focus on the end result which is the ultimate of fulfillment of destiny. A discovery of purpose gives you a focused life and with patience you will be able to keep your eyes on the fulfillment of that purpose. It is patience that will help you wait until you get your desired result which, in most cases, does not come easily as you may expect.

Donald Trump once said; ***"In the end, you're measured not by how much you undertake but by what you finally accomplish."***

Many times, starting something new requires a lot of sacrifices which include patiently waiting and delaying gratification until results begin to come. And in most cases that result will come bit by bit until the full delivery. But if focus is not maintained the end result may not be in view. It is patience that empowers focus and the end result will be obtained as you patiently endure (Hebrews 6:15)

Peace In Time Of Crisis

One of the issues that cannot be over emphasized in the pursuit of purpose is crisis. There are different angles to crisis depending on the name we give to it. In some cases, it may be called challenges, while in other cases, it is called adversity. Crisis is any circumstance that confronts people in order to delay or stop their advancement in the pursuit of an assignment.

There will always be something trying to stop the way against your advancement in life, because there is no challenge-free track on the path of destiny. To be able to keep going in spite of the oppositions, peace of mind is required. And this peace comes with a virtue of patience at work in man.

1 Peter 2:20;

...but if, when ye do well, and suffer for it, ye take it patiently, this is acceptable with God.

Suffering in this context connotes the crisis or challenges that one encounters on the way to fulfillment. To be patient at such a time is acceptable to God and with that understanding, peace of mind is guaranteed.

Romans 5:3-4;

And not only so, but we glory in tribulations also: knowing that tribulation worketh patience;

And patience, experience; and experience, hope:

The tribulations of life work patience. Therefore, you can rejoice in the midst of your crisis with an assurance of God's presence with you all the way.

Joy Of Harvest

There is what we call the joy of harvest and patience is the key to that joy. There is a planting season, there is the waiting season and there is the harvest season. In most cases, it is somehow painful during the planting and waiting, because, they are periods of sacrificing. And sacrifice will always cost us something. The time of discovery of purpose is like the time of planting of crops in the farm. There is need to wait for the period of time required for the crop to germinate and begin to yield harvest. That is the season that the purpose begins to see the light of the day and joy will naturally flow at that season.

Isaiah 9:3;

Thou hast multiplied the nation, and not increased the joy: they joy before thee according to the joy in harvest, and as men rejoice when they divide the spoil.

Every farmer rejoices and celebrates in harvest, but that joy of harvest is a product of the patience of the farmer to wait until harvest time. When harvest comes, the pains of the past seasons are no longer remembered. When you have an understanding of the fact that since your planting season is sure, harvest season is equally sure, that will energize and empower your patience.

A Living Hope

Hope means happy expectation of a positive outcome. It means full assurance of a glorious end result. However, it is patience that empowers hope and energizes us to wait in happy expectation until the end. When hope is lost along the line, fulfillment of destiny is hindered. There is need to keep hope alive and that will be made possible with the virtue of patience at work in you.

Roman 8:25;

But if we hope for that we see not, then do we with patience wait for it.

Patience is a major factor that engenders positive expectation of a glorious end.

Zeal For Continuity

There is power in continuity. It takes a continuous effort to get to the finishing line. There are many things in life that requires a daily commitment in order to accomplish a great result, but it takes grace of continuity to remain committed to such things. And that grace for continuity is a product of the virtue of patience at work in us.

The zeal needed to continue until the end result is accomplished comes with patience. Only those who continued patiently to the end can obtain the end result.

Mark 13:13;

And ye shall be hated of all men for my name's sake: but he that shall endure unto the end, the same shall be saved.

When you gain access to the virtue of patience, you will keep pressing until you arrive at the end result, because it is only those who press on that will finish the race. And it is only those who finish the race that will obtain the prize.

Press on with patience and you are sure to arrive at your destination. Patience is the greatest of all virtues.

HOW TO ACTIVATE THE VIRTUE OF PATIENCE

Patience is a virtue of an inestimable value, but it must be activated in order to become active in us as we seek to accomplish God's purpose in life. This virtue can be activated in the following ways;

The Holy Spirit

Patience is one of the fruits of the spirit. It is one of the virtues that come along with the in filling of the Holy Spirit in believers.

Galatians 5:22-23;

But the fruit of the Spirit is love, joy, peace, patience, kindness, goodness, faithfulness,

Gentleness and self-control. Against such things there is no law. (NIV)

When the Holy Spirit is actively working in you, patience, among others will be at work in you.

However, the presence of a gift in man is not equal to the operation of the gift. The fact that you have the fruit of the Spirit in you does not mean that it will work automatically. It must be activated to produce. And one major way to do that is to engage the help of the Holy Spirit in prayers.

In other words, as you pray in the spirit or pray in unknown tongues from time to time, you are activating the fruit of patience that is in you.

(Romans 8:26-27, Jude 20). Take the time to wait in God's presence to pray in the spirit from time to time so as to activate the virtue of patience that is already in you.

The Knowledge of God

Access to the knowledge of God is pivotal to activating the virtue of patience. When you have an understanding of who your God is and how powerful He is, you will not be in a hurry to get result. There is nothing done in a hurry that ends up well in many cases. Patience is required in every issue of life and the knowledge of God is what imparts that virtue into man.

He knowledge of God is pivotal to activating the virtue of patience. When you have an understanding of who your God is and how powerful He is, you will not be in a hurry to get result. There is nothing done in a hurry that ends up well in many cases. Patience is required in every issue of life and the knowledge of God is what imparts that virtue into man.

Isaiah 28:16;

Therefore thus saith the Lord GOD, Behold, I lay in Zion for a foundation, a stone, a tried stone, a precious corner stone, a sure foundation: he that believeth shall not make haste.

Jesus Christ is that sure foundation and your knowledge of Him will bring you to a level of believe in Him which will take haste and hurry away from your life. This is because exploits is the heritage of those who have the knowledge of God by the virtue of strength imparted by patience. (Daniel 11:32b)

When Job was facing the crisis of his life, he testified of his knowledge of his God and he was able to wait patiently until his change came.

Job 19:25;

For I know that my redeemer liveth, and that he shall stand at the latter day upon the earth:

Also, the great Apostle Paul affirmed his knowledge of God which was the key to his endurance until he finished his race on earth.

2 Timothy 1:12;

For the which cause I also suffer these things: nevertheless I am not ashamed: for I know whom I have believed, and am persuaded that he is able to keep that which

I have committed unto him against that day.

Your knowledge of God will help in activating the virtue of patience in you. Therefore, make the Word of God you daily companion so that you will increase in the knowledge of God. And the more of His knowledge you gain access to, the greater the working of His virtues in you.

Testimonies of Great Achievers

Every great achiever operates with the virtue of patience. As a matter of fact, patience is one of the keys to successful leadership and every one who has achieved greatness is automatically a leader. In other words, patience is required for successful achievement. Therefore, when you read the story of men with testimony of great achievement, you will discovered that one of the things that made them is the virtue of patience, that discovery will impart to you the same virtue which will help you to become a great achiever.

It was Benjamin Franklin that said; **"He who can have patience can have what he wills."**

When I read the stories of great men like some of those I have already made mention of in this book, I became very positive as I pursue my purpose. I discovered how many of them attained greatness from nothing, and how a great number of them became 'heroes' from 'zero', and from being 'Nobody' to 'Somebody'.

The story of Thomas Edison revealed how he made an outstanding achievement in life by patiently trying over and over again in an experiment.

Also, I read the story of Abraham Lincoln, one of the greatest presidents that have ruled America. I saw how that he made several attempts in try to lead at different levels in business and the politics of his country. He failed on several occasions and suffered business and career breakdowns. But Mr. Lincoln kept trying with patience until he emerged as the President of the United States of America.

Sam Walton, the founder of Wal-Mart, the largest retail business in the world with over 8,970 store worldwide and largest employer of labour in the world with over two million, two hundred people did it with patience. He started with only one store with borrowed money. Although his first store was closed down, he never gave up his dream and he became one of the wealthiest men in his days.

It is very important for you to know that every story of success has its paragraphs of failures. And every fabric of promotion has its threads of pain woven into it. Every road to victory has its own milestones of defeat. And every path to achievement is marked with bloodstains from the bruised knees and elbows of the champions in the moment of their fall.

Also, the bright lights of gain make sense only against the darkness of loss. Sweet wine is twice more delightful to the tongue that has known the taste of a bitter brew.

Oliver Goldsmith once said; **"Our greatest glory is not in never falling; but in rising up every time we fall."**

It takes the virtue of patience to keep rising up every time one falls, because failure is not fatal and success is not final. With ordinary talent and extraordinary perseverance, all things are attainable. The future is very bright and sure, but you need patience, perseverance and persistence to get there. I see you end your race on earth with the prize of a fulfilled destiny.

Hebrews 10:36;

For ye have need of patience, that, after ye have done the will of God, ye might receive the promise.

With patience, you are sure of finishing strong. I believe that God will help you to apply the principles that will establish this virtue in you as you pursue your purpose in life.

Anything is achievable with the right preparation and the right frame of mind. Through perseverance and self-discipline you can discover that you are closer to your goal than you think. It just takes one step at a time.

Ja-Nae Duane

Chapter 11: IT IS YOUR PROPHETIC ERA OF EXPLOITS

A day of darkness and of gloominess, a day of clouds and of thick darkness, as the morning spread upon the mountains: a great people and a strong; there hath not been ever the like, neither shall be any more after it, even to the years of many generations...

They shall run like mighty men; they shall climb the wall like men of war; and they shall march every one on his ways, and they shall not break their ranks:

Neither shall one thrust another; they shall walk every one in his path: and when they fall upon the sword, they shall not be wounded. - Joel 2:2, 7-8

We have come to the era of strange dimensions of impact and exploits for the church, and you are a candidate for this strange era as a Spirit-filled child of God. Anyone who is not a member of the body of Christ in this prophetic era of exploits will never taste of it.

That is the reason why I am emphasizing the need to be born again and filled with the Spirit of God because lasting exploits and greatness can only be found in the centre of God's plan and purpose for man.

Everything I have been sharing in this book from the beginning will only work effectively for the redeemed of the Lord, so it is never late to identify with Christ so that you can be part of the blessedness of a fulfilled destiny.

I have taken the time to share the story of great men in this book; a great number of them are believers who are doing exploits in life. Some of them are already dead, but their glory is still filling the earth as the water covers the sea.

This is because they discovered God's purpose and gave their lives to its pursuit until they arrived at the finish line. It then suffices to imply that impact and exploits in life begins with a discovery of divine purpose and tireless pursuit of same.

However, it is very important to know and understand the key factor for sustaining the exploits that God has reserved for His people this end time. This key factor is what everyone who has achieved any great thing in life used to keep the greatness alive and continuous.

Gratitude is the key. When you begin to celebrate God for anything, He will multiply it and enable you to get greater results. Gratitude is an expression of our appreciation to the source of exploits that we are privilege to do. God is the source of every great thing and we need to constantly return to Him in genuine appreciation so as to preserve the exploits and energize us to do more.

Gratitude is the attitude of thanksgiving and praise to God for everything about our lives.

Gratitude cannot fail because God expects it from us and He responds to it. God knows that we cannot on our own achieve anything without His help, so He wants us to acknowledge the fact that we have not gotten any result by our strength.

King David, the psalmist is a very good example of exploits through constant gratitude. The book of psalms is full of gratitude to God in thanksgiving and praise as documented by David. It is not a surprise that King David did great exploits that are still being remembered today.

Psalm 103:1-5;

Bless the LORD, O my soul: and all that is within me, bless his holy name.

Bless the LORD, O my soul, and forget not all his benefits:

Who forgiveth all thine iniquities; who healeth all thy diseases;

Who redeemeth thy life from destruction; who crowneth thee with lovingkindness and tender mercies;

Who satisfieth thy mouth with good things; so that thy youth is renewed like the eagle's.

King David attributed every exploits in his life to the faithfulness of God and in all the battles he fought, he never lost one. He is known to always rejoice in the Lord, which is an attitude of gratitude (Psalm 32:11)

Until you acknowledge the hand of God in your life in every situation as you rejoice always, you are not a candidate for exploits. You need to develop an attitude of gratitude, and give thanks for everything that happens to you, knowing that every step forward is a step toward achieving something bigger and better than your current situation.

Paul the great Apostle is another man known for an ever flowing attitude of gratitude, thanksgiving and praise. He suffered many things as he pursued God's purpose for his life, but all you hear from him from time to time is rejoice in the Lord always. (Philippians 4:4), rejoice evermore (1 Thessalonians 5:16). With this attitude of rejoicing, Paul did great exploits that are still speaking today.

When you appreciate God, He appreciates you. In other words, when you lift God up in praise, He lifts you up with His blessings.

Why is gratitude and rejoicing important in the pursuit of divine purpose?

The divine strength needed to pursue divine purpose is released through the act of rejoicing. No one can fulfill divine purpose in his own strength. (1

Samuel 2:9). We all need divine energy and it will come through rejoicing.

Nehemiah 8:10;

Then he said unto them, Go your way, eat the fat, and drink the sweet, and send portions unto them for whom nothing is prepared: for this day is holy unto our Lord: neither be ye sorry; for the joy of the Lord is your strength.

When you are rejoicing in the Lord, you are partaking of divine strength that you need to do exploits.

Another virtue of gratitude and rejoicing is divine presence. God can only be found in an atmosphere of joy and when you have access to His presence, every opposition on your way to your fulfillment will crumble.

Psalm 22:3;

But thou art holy, O thou that inhabitest the praises of Israel

---

When God's presence is released through praise, the hindrances to man's fulfillment will give way. Gratitude has the capacity of bringing down divine presence (Isaiah 64:1)

Also, kingdom stars and celebrities are made by gratitude and praise. This is because the fresh oil required for exploits is released through gratitude. That fresh oil is the anointing for exploits.

Psalm 92:1, 10;

It is a good thing to give thanks unto the LORD, and to sing praises unto thy name, O most High:

But my horn shalt thou exalt like the horn of an unicorn: I shall be anointed with fresh oil.

When you are giving God thanks and praise, you are gaining access to His fresh anointing that engenders exploits. God is interested in your fulfillment, but you have to submit to His ways by discovering and pursuing His purpose for your life.

You are a kingdom star and a kingdom celebrity. All you need to actualize this status is to pay full attention to all the truth I have shared in this book. Take every chapter serious because each one is like a rung on the ladder. To climb up, you must take your step a rung at a time until you find yourself at the top of the ladder.

You are meant for the top and the top is where you are going from now. See you at the top as you discover, pursue and fulfill your God given purpose on earth.

GET CONNECTED

In case you have read this book and you are yet to receive Jesus as your personal Lord and Savior, please, say these words as your act of submission to God's redemption plan:

Thank you Heavenly Father for sending Your Son Jesus to save me. Lord Jesus, I believe that you died and resurrected to save me, I ask that you come into my life today. Forgive me of my sin, cleanse me with your blood and accept me in the beloved. I confess you as my Lord and Savior today. Now I know that I am born again and saved from sin and the world. Thank you Lord for saving me. Amen.

I congratulate you for making this great decision today and I pray that you will not fall apart in your walk with God in this new-found faith in Christ.

If this book has been of great blessing to you, please write us through our emails or send SMS or give us a call through our phones numbers to share your testimonies. You can also connect with us through our Facebook pages and website.

Do not fail to recommend this book to other people as a way of being a blessing to them in contributing to the fulfillment of their God-ordained purposes in life.

In addition, we welcome your comments and views about the book so as to know how we can serve you and other people in a better way.

Thank you. We love you

Other Books By The Same Author

1. Become The Best! Release Your Potential

2. Dream Big and Succeed

3. Living Your Vision

4. Purpose Power Secrets

5. Your Dream Creates Your Future

About The Author

Sunday Adeniyi Ezekiel is an ordained Pastor, Insightful Teacher, Creative and Innovative Leadership Coach, with a visionary mandate to raise a people of impact and Exploits.

Ordained into an independent ministry by Bishop David Oyedepo of Living Faith Church a.k.a. Winners Chapel International after serving as a Pastor for some years in the headquarters in Canaan Land.

He is the President and Senior Pastor of DREAMERS WORLD CHRISTIAN CENTRE (a.k.a Faith Impact Chapel Int'l) Lagos, Nigeria.

As an astute business magnate with a passion to help people create lasting wealth, he is the co-founder, Executive Director and member of the Board of Directors of RICHLIFE COMMERCIAL AND LOGISTICTS LIMITED, a fast growing real estate company with two major brands namely RICHLIFE ESTATE AND GARDENS and RICHLIFE ROYAL CITY with over 500 network of Associates spread across Lagos, other parts of Nigeria and abroad.

He holds a Diploma in Public Accounting and Auditing from Kwara State Polytechnic, Ilorin and BSc in Business Administration from Lagos State University.

He is also a graduate of Leadership Diploma from Word of Faith Bible Institute (WOFBI) and Leadership Certificate from Daystar Leadership Academy (DLA), Lagos.

He is happily married to his lovely wife Helen who is a co-labourer in the work of the ministry. They are blessed with children; Oyindamola, Olamiposi and Olasurubomi.

www.ingramcontent.com/pod-product-compliance
Lightning Source LLC
Chambersburg PA
CBHW052307220526
45472CB00001B/15